THE
ULTIMATE
ALLERGY-FREE
COOKBOOK

OVER 150 EASY-TO-MAKE RECIPES THAT
CONTAIN NO MILK, EGGS, WHEAT, PEANUTS,
TREE NUTS, SOY, FISH, OR SHELLFISH

JUDI AND SHARI ZUCKER

SQUAREONE
PUBLISHERS

COVER DESIGNER: Jeannie Tudor
EDITOR: Marie Caratozzolo
TYPESETTER: Gary A. Rosenberg
INTERIOR ART: Cathy Morrison
ART ON PAGE 147: Vicki Chelf

Square One Publishers
115 Herricks Road
Garden City Park, NY 11040
(516) 535-2010 • (877) 900-BOOK
www.squareonepublishers.com

Library of Congress Cataloging-in-Publication Data
Zucker, Judi.
    The ultimate allergy-free cookbook : over 150 easy-to-make recipes that
contain no milk, eggs, wheat, peanuts, tree nuts, soy, fish, or shellfish /
Judi and Shari Zucker.
      pages cm
    Includes index.
    ISBN 978-0-7570-0397-4 (pbk.)
    1. Food allergy—Diet therapy—Recipes. I. Zucker, Shari. II. Title.
    RC588.D53Z84 2014
    641.5'6318—dc23
                                                                      2014007777

Printed in the United States of America

10   9   8   7   6   5   4   3   2   1

CONTENTS

We would like to dedicate this book

With heartfelt love and gratitude to our parents,

Irwin and Devra Zucker.

You are—and have always been—our true inspiration.

ACKNOWLEDGMENTS

Through our work with Square One Publishers, we have come to know three people who are now like family to us. They are publisher Rudy Shur, senior editor Marie Caratozzolo, and public relations/marketing director Anthony Pomes. We are very grateful to them all.

Rudy, you are a true visionary. Your commitment to educating others on the benefits of a healthful lifestyle through the publication of best-selling books is truly commendable. We thank you for all of your encouragement and support with our projects. Marie, you are the best editor we have ever worked with. We appreciate your attention to detail and to all of your excellent suggestions in making our book the best that it could be. We are so fortunate to work with you.

Anthony, what an extraordinary person you are—someone who always goes above and beyond. You are the consummate professional, a jack of all trades with a heart of gold! We will never forget how, after the publication of our last book, you accompanied us on a publicity tour throughout New York City during sweltering 90-degree days. Despite the oppressive heat, you stayed dressed in

a suit and tie while taking us from one radio station and television studio to another. You somehow managed to cart all of our stuff—water bottles, purses, and boxes of cooking supplies—as we made our way through the streets of Manhattan. (All while making sure our hair and makeup looked just right.) You were our body guard, publicist, and friend. We love you, Anthony. You make every challenge an "adventure."

Nothing can be more important than the love of family, and we are very fortunate to be blessed with such love. To our terrific husbands, Daniel and Chris, you are inspirations to us every day. And to our children—Max, Miles, Mattea, Taryn, and Tanner—you are true blessings! We are so proud of all of you and appreciate the many ways you show your love and never-ending support.

Finally, we would like to offer a very special acknowledgment to our parents. Mom, thanks to you and your "less than adequate" cooking skills, we were determined at an early age to learn our way around the kitchen. By the time we were eleven, we had begun preparing meals for the family. This led to our discovery of nutritious food choices and the commitment to a healthy lifestyle. Encouraging us to share our recipes with others inspired us to become cookbook authors—a vocation that has proven to be a joyful labor of love.

Dad, as the mastermind behind "The Double Energy Twins," we owe you a very special debt of gratitude. Being a PR genius, you have always come up with creative ways to help us in our careers. You are a man of great integrity who also has a genuinely kind heart. While we were growing up, you often reminded us that "It doesn't cost anything to be nice." Well, Dad, you are the nicest man we know—a true role model. Together with Mom, you are the best parents anyone could ever ask for. We love you both very much!

Here's 2 Health!
Judi and Shari

INTRODUCTION

With an alarming increase in the number of people diagnosed with food allergies—the majority being children under the age of eighteen—supermarket shelves are looking much different than they did in the recent past. In an effort to meet consumer needs, stores now offer a wide variety of allergen-free products—snack foods like chips and crackers, sweet treats like cookies and cakes, fresh and frozen prepared foods, and the list goes on. While this certainly seems like a positive step in catering to an obvious demand, it also comes with a possible downside.

The problem is that the majority of commercially made products, although allergen free, are often nutrient free, as well. They tend to be highly processed and loaded with undesirable, health-compromising ingredients like refined sugar, trans fats, preservatives, and artificial colorings and flavorings. Anyone dealing with a food allergy knows that avoiding the problematic ingredient is critical; but maintaining overall good health through a nutritious diet is just as important. So how can you serve food that is not only safe to eat, but nutritionally sound as well? The answer lies in the pages of this book.

The Ultimate Allergy-Free Cookbook provides over 150 tasty vegetarian/vegan recipes that are free of the top eight allergenic foods according to the current assessment of the United States Food and Drug Administration. That means each recipe is made without eggs, cow's milk, peanuts, tree nuts, wheat, soy, fish, and shellfish. They are also free of gluten and refined white sugar. (Very few allergy-free cookbooks can make this claim. Often, the recipes are free of one or two of the top allergenic ingredients, but not all of them.)

As an added bonus, the dishes in this book are wholesome and nutritious—rich in whole grains and fiber, and low in fat and calories. They also call for ingredients that are readily available and affordable, and best of all, they are simple to prepare. Easy-to-follow step-by-step directions guarantee that even the most inexperienced cooks will enjoy successful results.

Perhaps most important, everything tastes good! After all, even the most nutritious foods aren't beneficial if no one eats them. That's why you'll find that the dishes in this book—the soups and salads, the smoothies and snacks, as well as the entrées, side dishes, and desserts—are tasty and satisfying. Your family will enjoy eating them, and you will feel good about serving them.

Along with the recipes, *The Ultimate Allergy-Free Cookbook* also offers a wealth of information and support for anyone living with food allergies. It shares important guidelines for setting up an allergen-free kitchen, instructions for reading food labels, and tips for avoiding cross-contamination of allergenic ingredients. A comprehensive table of ingredient substitutions provides options for a number of common food allergens. With it, you will be able to easily adjust most recipes to suit your particular needs. This book also discusses healthful food options, including the importance of choosing organic products and avoiding genetically modified foods, which can be especially harmful to those with food allergies. Also included is an extensive resource section that provides an invaluable listing of informative websites, organizations, recommended products, and reliable manufacturers that support an allergen-free lifestyle.

This truly is the *ultimate* allergy-free cookbook. It doesn't matter which of the top allergenic foods you must avoid, or if the allergy is mild or severe. You can serve all of the delectable dishes in this book without fear of a reaction. Best of all, the recipes are not just for those with allergies—everyone can enjoy them.

1

Allergies on the Rise

Over 15 million people in the United States suffer from food allergies, with the highest incidence among children under eighteen years old. And the number continues to climb. According to a recent study by the Centers for Disease Control, food allergies have nearly doubled over the past ten years—and there is no definitive reason why.

Heredity is believed to be the primary cause of food allergies. Chances are one in three that a child will develop an allergy if one parent has an allergy of any type. These odds increase to seven in ten if both parents have allergies. But why the sudden increase?

A growing number of researchers suggest that this noticeable rise may be due to what is called the *hygiene hypothesis*—our tendency toward "clean living." We strive for an antiseptic, dirt-free world; one in which our immune systems no longer have to fight germs the way they used to. Medications and antibiotics have taken further burden off our immune systems, which have shifted their focus from fighting infections to developing more allergic tendencies, such as

viewing harmless proteins in foods as harmful invaders, overreacting to them, and then causing an allergenic response. Since more people are developing allergies and more allergic couples are having children, the increase in the number of affected children is naturally on the rise.

Introducing known allergenic foods into a child's diet too early may be another cause of the rising allergy rates—a theory that has proven controversial. And recently, an interesting study conducted at Italy's University of Florence indicated that poor dietary choices, such as those associated with the western diet, may also be a contributing factor to a child's susceptibility to allergies, as well as obesity and a number of other conditions and illnesses. Researchers compared the effects of the fiber-rich diet of fourteen children from a rural African village in Burkina Faso to the more-westernized diets of fifteen children from Florence. The African children ate mostly grains, beans, nuts, and vegetables that had been raised near their homes, while the diet of the Italian children included more meat, fat, and sugar. Study results showed that the digestive systems of the African children were flourishing with "good" bacteria and an abundance of beneficial fatty acids, which are associated with a reduced risk of obesity, inflammation, asthma, eczema, and other allergic reactions. By comparison, the systems of the Italian children had nowhere near the same beneficial environment—a condition that could lead to allergies and other inflammatory diseases.

There's no question that the number of people developing food allergies is growing. While strict avoidance of the offending food may be the only way to prevent a reaction, eating a healthy, nutritious diet may be another important factor in reducing the risk that can lead to allergies.

FOOD ALLERGY OR FOOD INTOLERANCE?

What exactly is a food allergy? Is it the same as food intolerance? Although both involve food sensitivities, these two conditions are different.

A *food allergy* occurs when the body's immune system overreacts to a food, believing it is harmful. To protect itself, the immune system mistakenly produces antibodies called *immunoglobulin E* (IgE). These antibodies cause the body to generate chemicals called *histamines*, which can cause an allergic response. This response can range from minor skin irritations like an itchy rash or stuffy nose to more serious respiratory problems, including life-threatening *anaphylaxis*. Signs of anaphylaxis, which usually occur within minutes after exposure to the allergen, typically include difficulty breathing and swallowing, and swelling of the lips, tongue, and throat. Early administration of epinephrine (available in an injectable "pen") is critical for successful treatment.

A *food intolerance* is similar to an allergy in that it causes an adverse reaction to a food; but unlike an allergy, it does not involve the immune system. Symptoms of food intolerance—often headaches and digestive issues—also tend to be less severe and non-life threatening. Although many foods can cause an intolerance, the most common offenders include *lactose*, a sugar found in milk and most dairy products; *salicylates*, a natural chemical contained in a variety of fruits and vegetables; *amines*, a chemical produced during the fermentation of wine and the ripening of certain foods; and *glutamate*, an amino acid in foods containing protein. The popular flavor enhancer monosodium glutamate (MSG) is the sodium salt of glutamate and a common cause of sensitivity.

Celiac disease, also known as *gluten intolerance* or *celiac sprue*, is a digestive condition that, although not considered an allergy, involves an immune system response. For a person with celiac, antibodies attack the lining of the small intestine when gluten is present. The lining becomes inflamed and is unable to absorb nutrients and minerals from food. A gluten-free diet—avoidance of all products containing wheat, rye, spelt, kamut, triticale, and barley—is the only treatment for this condition.

As stated earlier, food allergies are more common in children than adults. The good news is that the majority of affected children will outgrow them.

OFFENDING FOODS

Unlike many non-food allergies, which can be treated with medication, there is no cure for food allergies. Strict avoidance of the offending food is the only way to prevent a reaction. The eight foods that trigger most allergic responses are peanuts, tree nuts, cow's milk and other dairy products, eggs, wheat, soy, fish, and crustacean shellfish. Children are more likely to suffer from allergics due to milk, eggs, and peanuts, while adults tend to be more allergic to fish and shellfish. Let's take a closer look at these highly allergenic foods.

Peanuts

Actually legumes (not nuts), peanuts are a growing cause of allergic reactions in children. According to a recent survey that appeared in *The Journal of Allergy and Clinical Immunology,* the number of children with peanut allergies more than tripled between 1997 and 2008. Nearly half of these children are also allergic to tree nuts. For many, a peanut allergy is a lifelong concern—only about 20 percent of children outgrow it.

An allergic reaction to peanuts can be mild or severe depending on the sensitivity of the individual. Even an extremely small amount can cause serious life-threatening anaphylaxis in some people.

It is obvious that peanut butter and any food or product that includes the word "peanut" indicates that it contains peanut protein, making the product easy to avoid. Sometimes, however, peanuts are sold as "beer nuts" or "monkey nuts," which are not as obvious. It is very important to read food labels to determine if the product contains peanut protein, which can be found in a number of unlikely sources. (See "Guide to Avoiding Food Allergens" on page 10.)

Tree Nuts

Approximately 1 percent of children in North America are allergic to tree nuts. Brazil nuts, almonds, cashews, chestnuts, walnuts, pecans, hazelnuts, macadamias, pistachios, and pine nuts are common tree nut varieties, but they are not the only ones.

Allergic reactions to tree nuts, as with peanuts, are generally lifelong and can be severe and even life-threatening. For the most part, people who are allergic to one tree nut are not usually allergic to all varieties. They may, however, be allergic to one or even a few others. They are also at greater risk for developing peanut allergies. For this reason—as well as the possibility of cross-contamination during the manufacturing process—most doctors advise that if you are allergic to one tree nut, it is best to simply avoid all nuts, and peanuts, too.

What about coconuts? Although the FDA considers coconut to be a tree nut (for food labeling purposes), technically it is *not* a nut; it is a seed. Coconut allergies are actually very rare, and most people with tree nut allergies are able to eat coconut without having an adverse reaction. So before eliminating coconut from your diet, first discuss this possibility with your doctor.

Also bear in mind that although chestnuts fall into the tree nut category, water chestnuts do not. Water chestnuts are the edible portion of a plant root, and safe for anyone with tree nut allergies. Nutmeg is also safe. Although it includes the word "nut" in its name, nutmeg is actually the fragrant seed of a topical tree.

Like peanuts, many foods that contain tree nuts are obvious, but there are many unexpected sources as well. A growing number of commercial products like salad dressings, cereals, meatless burgers, and pie crusts contain tree nuts. And many ethnic cuisines, such as Greek and Chinese, are famous for dishes and pastries that contain nuts. Reading food labels and maintaining an awareness of the possible presence of food allergens in unexpected sources is critical. For details, see the listing on page 11.

Milk

An allergy to cow's milk is the most common childhood food allergy, affecting approximately 2.5 percent of children under age three. Most affected children develop the allergy during their first year. *Casein,* the protein in cow's milk, is the most common culprit, although most children who are allergic to cow's milk are also allergic to goat's milk and sheep's milk. Some are also allergic to soymilk.

Typical symptoms of a milk allergy, which usually occur shortly after consumption, include vomiting, hives, and gastrointestinal distress. These reactions can be mild or severe, although generally they are not life threatening. On a positive note, many children outgrow milk allergies by the time they are three or four years old. By age eighteen, most are no longer affected.

Along with cheese, butter, yogurt, and ice cream, milk is found in a tremendous number of processed foods and baked goods. When checking ingredient labels, keep an eye out for the words "whey" and "casein," which indicate "milk." There are many other foods that may contain milk or other dairy products and must be avoided (see the list on page 12).

When eating in Mexican or Italian restaurants, where cheese is a popular ingredient and could possibly cross-contaminate the food, be especially careful. And be careful at delis, where cold cuts may be cut on the same slicer used for cheese. Also be aware that lactose-free milks and other lactose-free products still contain milk solids and are not meant for anyone with a milk allergy. They are intended for those with lactose intolerance.

Eggs

An egg allergy follows milk as the second most-common childhood food allergy. It usually begins when a child is very young, and is often gone by age seven or eight. The allergic reaction (more often to the egg white than the yolk) generally starts within minutes or hours after eating eggs and doesn't last more than a day. Typical reactions include hives or skin rash, runny nose, sneezing, watery eyes, coughing, breathing difficulties, vomiting, and diarrhea. Most children will experience more than one of these reactions, which could be mild or severe. In very rare cases, life-threatening anaphylaxis can occur.

Eggs aren't just found in omelets. They are contained in many prepared foods, baked goods, and processed products. And don't be fooled into thinking that commercial egg substitutes found in the refrigerated section of your grocery store are egg-free. Most contain egg whites. There are, however, vegan egg-free substitutes that come in powdered form and are safe to use.

It's important to be aware of the many hidden egg sources—like pretzels, dinner rolls, and loaves of bread, which are sometimes coated with egg wash for a glossy shine, or that cappuccino, whose foamy topping may contain egg. Check the listings on page 13 for other foods and ingredients to avoid.

Wheat

Another common food allergy, especially among children, is caused by the protein found in wheat. This allergy usually develops when a child is between six months and two years of age. Most children outgrow it by age five. Like many allergic reactions, symptoms of wheat allergy usually occur a few minutes to a few hours after eating the problem food. Typical symptoms, which can be mild or severe, include hives, itchy eyes, difficulty breathing, nausea or vomiting, and diarrhea. In some severe cases, anaphylaxis can occur.

CROSS-CONTAMINATION CONCERNS

Thanks to the FALCPA, food manufacturers must clearly state in plain English the presence of any of the top allergenic foods on product labels. (See "Food Labeling" on page 9.) Currently, however, manufacturers are *not* required to state if the food was processed in a facility that processes other allergenic foods—where the possibility of cross-contamination is a real concern.

Fortunately, although they are not required to do so, a growing number of manufacturers are voluntarily including this information on labels. The note can state, for example, that the product was made in a "wheat-free" or "dairy-free" facility. Or as a warning, it can say that the product "may contain wheat" or that it was "processed in a facility that also processes peanuts."

When checking ingredient lists, be sure to also look for this additional note. If there isn't one, don't assume the product is safe. If there is any question regarding the possibility of a product's cross-contact with an allergenic food, contact the manufacturer directly.

Anyone with a wheat allergy must avoid all products made from wheat. It is important to also stay away from products made from spelt and kamut—two grains that are closely related to wheat. (For a detailed list of products to avoid, see page 14.) People with wheat allergies can, however, eat other grains, including amaranth, barley, buckwheat, corn, millet, oats, quinoa, rice, rye, and teff.

A wheat allergy is sometimes confused with celiac disease, also known as *gluten intolerance*. As mentioned earlier, those with celiac disease cannot eat *any* product that contains gluten, which is found not only in wheat but also in rye, kamut, spelt, and barley. Unlike a wheat allergy, which is often outgrown, celiac disease is a lifelong condition and, unfortunately, the number of people who have it is on the rise.

Although it is not considered an allergy, celiac disease does involve an immune system response that targets and damages the lining of the small intestine. For this reason, the recipes in this book—in addition to being free of the eight top food allergens—are also gluten-free, making them safe for those with celiac disease.

Soy

Like peanuts, soybeans are classified as legumes. Childhood allergies to soybeans and soy products are about half as common as peanut allergies. In infants, rashes and digestive problems are often signs of a soy allergy, while toddlers and older children tend to experience runny nose, watery eyes, wheezing, and other cold-like symptoms. These allergic reactions are generally mild in nature; however, anaphylaxis can occur in rare cases. Although most children eventually outgrow a soy allergy by age ten, for some, it continues into adulthood.

Because soybeans are so inexpensive, a growing number of food manufacturers have begun replacing more costly ingredients with soy products. For instance, the peanut oil once used in many brands of peanut butter has been replaced with cheaper vegetable oil blends that often contain soy oil. Some herbal teas contain soy as a filler. And even fresh produce is sometimes sprayed with soy oil to give it an eye-appealing shine. (Buying certified organic produce is one way to avoid this particular problem.)

Seafood— Fish and Shellfish

Seafood allergies affect approximately 7 million Americans. Although this type of allergy is more common in adults than children, it can occur at any age; and for most, it is a lifelong condition. Allergic reactions usually begin a few minutes to a few hours after consuming the food, and may include tingling or swelling of the lips, tongue, or throat; dizziness; hives; difficulty breathing; nausea; and diarrhea. A severe reaction can cause anaphylaxis.

Salmon, tuna, and halibut are among the fish (with fins and backbones) that are considered the most allergenic. As for shellfish, which fall into two categories—crustaceans and mollusks—only crustaceans are considered major food allergens. Shrimp, lobster, and crab are among the top offenders. Because mollusks, such as clams, oys-

TAKING PRECAUTIONS

If you, your child, or anyone else in your home has a food allergy—especially a severe one—taking the following precautions can help prevent potential problems.

✓ If you don't know ALL of the ingredients in a prepared food or food product, do not serve it.

✓ Whenever possible, prepare meals at home, where you are certain of the ingredients.

✓ If possible, do not keep the problem food in the home.

✓ If you keep the allergen food in your home, be careful of cross-contamination. Don't use the same utensils, cookware, cutting boards, etc. to prepare allergenic and non-allergenic foods. At places like ice cream parlors, be cautious of cross-contact that can result from shared scoops.

✓ Read food labels carefully for the presence of allergens (see the table beginning on page 10). Some food manufacturers label their products to verify that they were prepared or packed in an allergen-free (or non allergen-free) environment. If there is any question regarding the possibility of a product's cross-contact with an allergenic food, contact the manufacturer directly.

✓ If your child is allergic, be sure to alert everyone he or she comes in contact with—teachers, school cafeteria staff, servers at restaurants, parents of playmates, babysitters—about the allergy.

✓ Make allergen-free snacks and treats for your child to take to parties and play dates.

✓ In cases of severe allergies, keep epinephrine (EpiPen, Twinject) accessible at all times.

ters, and scallops, are not considered major food allergens, they do not have to be listed on ingredient labels. (See "Food Labeling" below for more information.) If you have an allergic reaction to crustacean shellfish, the doctor may advise you to avoid mollusks as well. (An extensive list of fish and shellfish to avoid appears on pages 16 and 17.)

In addition to reading ingredient labels and knowing which foods to avoid, it is also a good idea to steer clear of seafood restaurants, where cross-contamination can easily involve a non-fish dish. And watch out for fried foods—many restaurants use the same oil to fry both seafood and non-seafood dishes. It is also important to be aware that Asian restaurants often flavor their dishes with fish-based sauces, so be very careful when ordering.

The only sure way to prevent an allergic food reaction is to avoid the problem food. For this reason, it is very important to be aware of these foods and ingredients, which are sometimes "hidden" under unfamiliar names or sources on food labels. For a detailed list, see "Guide to Avoiding Food Allergens" beginning on page 10.

FOOD LABELING

On January 1, 2006, the Food Allergen Labeling and Consumer Protection Act (FALCPA) took effect. This act requires that foods containing one or more of the major food allergens (milk, eggs, peanuts, tree nuts, soy, wheat, fish, and crustacean shellfish) must state the allergen clearly and in plain language on the label.

The specific allergen may appear on the ingredient list or it may be stated in parentheses after the listed food source, such as "albumin (egg)." It may also appear in a section near the ingredient list after the word "contains" (e.g. "Contains soy and wheat."). These allergens must be listed if they are present in any amount, and if they are in spice blends, colorings, flavorings, preservatives, or any other additives. Additionally, manufacturers must list the *specific* nut (e.g. almonds, macadamias) or seafood (e.g., salmon, shrimp, lobster) that is contained in the product.

FALCPA has certainly made label reading easier for the millions of Americans living with food allergies. Be aware, however, that *these requirements do not cover all foods*. For instance, packaged take-out food from restaurants, fast-food establishments, and street vendors that is provided in response to a person's order is not required to follow FALCPA guidelines. This is also the case for prepared foods sold in grocery stores and delis. Other products that are not covered by FALCPA include fresh fruits and vegetables, highly refined oils, and beer and other alcoholic beverages.

Kosher products are also exempt from FALCPA guidelines. And keep in mind that locally made and distributed foods may not be in full compliance. It is also very important to remember that these labeling requirements are for American food products only. Foods that are packaged in Canada and other countries are not required to list allergens as clearly (or at all). An allergen such as soy, for example, may be contained in a product, yet "hidden" under an ingredient such as "natural flavors." The message here is clear: *Always* check labels carefully for food allergens, including those that are possibly hidden. (See the "Guide to Avoiding Food Allergens" beginning on page 10.) If you are not 100-percent certain of the ingredients in a product, avoid it.

Guide to Avoiding Food Allergens

The following table presents the eight common food allergens along with many of the foods, products, and ingredients that may cause an allergic reaction. As discussed in the section on "Food Labeling" (page 9), most—*but not all*—foods packaged in the United States must clearly state if the product contains any of these allergens. *Always check food labels carefully.* And be aware that manufacturers often change product ingredients without notice, so never skip reading labels of familiar products because you "know" what they contain. It is important to check labels with every purchase.

Peanuts

FOODS / INGREDIENTS TO AVOID	Anything with the word "peanut" (brittle, butter, etc.)		
	Arachis	Goober peas	Monkey nuts
	Arachis hypogaea	Goobers	Nu-Nuts
	Arachis oil	Ground nuts	Nut pieces
	Artificial nuts	Hydrolyzed peanut protein	Nutmeat
	Beer nuts	Hypogaeic acid	Peanut oil (cold-pressed, expeller-pressed, extruded)
	Crushed nuts	Mandelonas	
	Earth nuts	Mixed nuts	

MAY CONTAIN PEANUT PROTEIN	Artificial and natural flavorings		
	Baked goods (cookies, cakes, pastries, breads)		
	Ethnic food/dishes: African, Asian, Mexican, and especially Chinese, Indian, Indonesian, Thai, and Vietnamese		
	Candy	Enchilada sauce	Marzipan
	Chili	Fried foods	Mole sauce
	Chocolate	Granola bars	Nougat
	Crumb/streusel toppings	Hydrolyzed plant protein	Pie crusts
	Egg rolls	Hydrolyzed vegetable protein	Trail mix

IMPORTANT INFORMATION	* According to the FDA, studies have shown that most allergic individuals can eat purified or highly refined peanut oil (not cold-pressed, extruded, or expeller-pressed) without a reaction. *Always check with your doctor first.*

Tree Nuts

FOODS/ INGREDIENTS TO AVOID			
Almonds	Heartnuts	Nut oils	
Anacardium nuts	Hickory nuts	Nut paste	
Artificial nuts	Indian nuts (pine nuts)	Nut pieces	
Beechnuts	Japanese walnuts	Nutella spread	
Brazil nuts	Lychee nuts (lichee, litchi)	Pecans	
Bush nuts	Macadamia nuts	Pesto	
Butternuts	Marzipan	Pili nuts	
Cashews	Mashuga nuts	Pine nuts (pignoli, pigñolia, pignons, pinions, piñons, Indian nuts)	
Chestnuts	Nangai nuts		
Chinquapins	Nougat		
Coconuts (see Important Information below)	Nu-Nuts		
	Nut butters	Pistachios	
Filberts	Nut extracts, natural	Pralines	
Gianduia chocolate	Nut meal	Shea nuts	
Ginkgo nuts	Nut meats	Walnuts	
Hazelnuts	Nut milks		

MAY CONTAIN TREE NUTS

Artificial and natural flavorings

Baked goods (cookies, cakes, pastries, breads, etc.)

Baking mixes (pancake, biscuit, cookie, cake, etc.)

Barbecue sauce	Granola bars	Nut distillates/ alcoholic extract
Black walnut hull extract	Ice cream, frozen desserts	Nut extracts, artificial
	Ice cream toppings	
Breading	Meat-free burgers	Pie crusts
Cereals	Mortadella luncheon meat (may contain pistachios)	Salads
Crackers		Salad dressings
Crumb/streusel toppings		Trail mixes

IMPORTANT INFORMATION

* Although the coconut is considered a tree nut by the FDA, it is actually a seed— and coconut allergies are very rare. Most people with tree nut allergies are able to eat coconut without having an adverse reaction. *Always check with your doctor first.*

* Unlike chestnuts, which are considered tree nuts, water chestnuts come from a plant root and are safe to eat.

* Although nutmeg sounds like a nut, it is the fragrant seed of a tropical tree and safe for those with nut allergies.

Milk (Cow's)

FOODS/ INGREDIENTS TO AVOID	Milk, all forms (dry, condensed, evaporated, low-fat, nonfat, skim, solids)		
	Acidophilus milk	Ghee	Milk fat
	Butter	Half-and-Half	Milk protein hydrolysate
	Butter acid	Hydrolysates	Nisin preparation
	Butter fat	Ice cream	Nougat
	Butter esters	Ice milk	Pudding
	Buttermilk	Lactaid	Quark
	Casein/caseinates (all forms)	Lactalbumin	Recaldent
	Cheese	Lactalbumin phosphate	Rennet
	Cottage cheese	Lactate solids	Sherbet
	Cream	Lactitol monohydrate	Simplesse
	Cream sauces		Sour cream
	Cream soups	Lactoferrin	Sour milk solids
	Curds	Lactoglobulin	Tagatose
	Custard	Lactose	Whey
	Dairy product solids	Lactulose	Whey protein hydrolysate
	Diacetyl	Lactyc yeast	Whipped cream
	Galactose	Margarine (except pareve)	Yogurt

MAY CONTAIN MILK	Artificial and natural flavorings		
	Baked goods (cookies, pastries, breads, etc.)		
	Baking mixes (pancake, biscuit, cookie, cake, etc.)		
	Butter flavor, artificial	Lactic acid	Nisin
	Caramel candy	Lactic acid starter culture	Nondairy products
	Caramel flavoring	Luncheon meats, hot dogs, sausage	Nougat
	Chocolate		Rice cheese
	High protein flour	Margarine	Soy cheese

IMPORTANT INFORMATION	* Most people who are allergic to cow's milk, also experience reactions from goat's milk and sheep's milk.

Eggs

Foods/ Ingredients to Avoid	Anything with the word "egg" (roll, nog, etc.)	

Albumin (albumen)	Hollandaise sauce	Ovotransferrin
Apovitellin	Livetin	Ovovitelia
Dried egg	Lysozyme	Ovovitellin
Egg substitutes (unless vegan)	Mayonnaise	Powdered egg
	Meringue	Silici albuminate
Egg solids	Meringue powder	Simplesse
Egg whites	Ovalbumin	Surimi (imitation crabmeat)
Eggnog	Ovoglobulin	
Fat substitutes	Ovomucin	Vitellin
Globulin	Ovomucoid	

May Contain Egg	Artificial and natural flavorings
	Most baked goods (cookies, cakes, pastries, etc.)
	Most custards and puddings

Lecithin	Noodles	Pasta
Marzipan	Nougat	

Important Information

* Eggs from ducks, turkeys, geese, quail, etc. are characteristically cross-reactive with chicken eggs and should be avoided.

* Be aware that egg wash is often used to add shine to pretzels, breads, rolls, and other baked goods.

* Eggs and egg derivatives may be contained in the foamy toppings of cappuccinos and other specialty coffees.

Wheat

**FOODS/
INGREDIENTS
TO AVOID**

Flour (all-purpose, bread, cake, durum, enriched, pastry, self-rising, stone-ground, steel-ground, whole wheat)

Wheat (berries, bran, germ, gluten, malt, starch, sprouts)

Beer	Fu	Semolina
Bran	Germ	Shoyu soy sauce
Bulgur (bulghur)	Gluten	Spelt
Bread crumbs	Hydrolyzed wheat protein	Sprouted wheat
Cereal extract	Kamut	Tabbouleh
Club wheat	Malt, malt extract	Triticale
Couscous	Matzoh (matza, matzah, matzo, matsoh)	Triticum
Cracker meal		Triticosecale
Crackers	Matzoh meal	Vital wheat gluten
Durum	Noodles	Wheat bran hydrolysate
Einkorn	Pasta	Wheat germ oil
Emmer	Seitan	Wheatgrass
Farina		Wheat protein isolate

**MAY CONTAIN
WHEAT**

Artificial and natural flavorings

Most baked goods (bread, cookies, crackers etc.)

Most baking mixes (pancake, biscuit, cookie, cake, etc.); cereals; pie crusts

Caramel color	Maltodextrin	Tamari soy sauce (see Important Information below)
Dextrin	Monosodium glutamate (MSG)	
Food starch (gelatinized, modified, vegetable)	Oats (see Important Information below)	Teriyaki sauce
Glucose syrup		Textured vegetable protein
Hydrolyzed vegetable protein	Soy sauce	Vegetable gum
	Surimi (imitation crab)	

**IMPORTANT
INFORMATION**

* Oats and oat flour are often processed in facilities that also handle wheat (and other gluten-containing grains like rye and barley), so cross-contamination may occur. Be sure to purchase varieties that are labeled wheat- or gluten-free.

*Tamari is traditionally a Japanese wheat-free soy sauce. Be aware, however, that tamari varieties made with wheat are now available, so read labels carefully.

Soy

FOODS/ INGREDIENTS TO AVOID	Anything with the word "soy" (beans, oil, sauce)		
	Bean curd	Nimame	Soybean paste
	Bean skin	Okara	Supro
	Edamame	Olean	Tamari soy sauce
	Hydrolyzed soy protein	Shoyu soy sauce	Tempeh
	Imitation bacon bits	Soy isoflavones	Teriyaki sauce
	Kinako flour	Soy protein concentrate	Textured vegetable protein
	Kouridofu	Soy protein isolate	Tofu
	Kyodofu	Soya, soya flour	Tofutti
	Lecithin	Soybean curd	Yakidofu
	Miso	Soybean granules	Yuba
	Natto		

MAY CONTAIN SOY	Artificial and natural flavorings
	Asian dishes
	Manufactured food products (see Important Information below)

Bouillon (liquid, cubes powder)	Hydrolyzed plant or vegetable protein	Vegetable gum
	Vegetable broth	Vegetable starch

IMPORTANT INFORMATION	* Soy is found in most manufactured food products. It is commonly used as an inexpensive filler, an emulsifier, and as a binding agent for "natural flavors."
	* Although purified soy oil and vegetable oil are supposed to be safe, be very careful. Numerous adverse reactions (some severe) have been reported after their use.

Shellfish

FOODS/ INGREDIENTS TO AVOID	**Crustaceans** *Considered major allergens*		

	Barnacles
	Crab
	Crayfish (crawdad,
	   crawfish, ecrevisse)
	Krill
		Lobster (langouste,
		   langoustine,
		   Moreton,
		   bay bugs,
		   tomalley)
			Prawns
			Shrimp (crevette,
			   scampi)

Mollusks *Not considered major allergens (see Important Information below)*

Abalone
Clams
  (cherrystone,
  geoduck,
  littleneck, top
  neck, steamers,
  mahoganies,
  pismo, quahog)
	Cockles
	Cuttlefish
	Limpet (lapas,
	  opihi)
	Mussels
	Octopus
	Oysters
		Periwinkle
		Scallops
		Sea cucumber
		Sea urchin
		Snails (escargot)
		Squid (calamari)
		Whelk

MAY CONTAIN
SHELLFISH
	Bouillabaisse
	Chowder
	Cuttlefish ink
	Fish stock
		Glucosamine
		  seafood flavoring
		  (e.g. crab or
		  clam extract)
			Sashimi
			Surimi
			Sushi

IMPORTANT INFORMATION	* Shellfish fall into two categories—crustaceans and mollusks. Only crustaceans are considered major food allergens. For this reason, FALCPA does not require mollusks to be listed on ingredient labels. *Always check with your doctor first.*

Fish

FOODS/ INGREDIENTS TO AVOID	Any vertebrate fish with fins (salmon, tuna, cod, bass swordfish, etc.)		
	Caviar (fish eggs)	Sashimi	Sushi
	Fish gelatin	Surimi (imitation crabmeat)	Worcestershire sauce (contains anchovies)
	Roe (fish eggs)		
MAY CONTAIN FISH	Caesar salad (some contain anchovies)		
	Caesar salad dressing		
IMPORTANT INFORMATION	* Some individuals with a fish allergy may be able to tolerate fish oil supplements. *Always check with your doctor first.*		

KEEPING IT ALLERGEN-FREE AND HEALTHY

Let's face it. With grocery store shelves filled with commercially prepared foods that are highly processed, calorie-laden, and often loaded with sugar, salt, trans fats, preservatives, food colorings, and other undesirable ingredients, it can be a real challenge to find healthy choices. And it can be even more challenging to find healthy foods that are also allergen-free.

For this reason, preparing your own dishes whenever possible is highly recommended. It puts you in control of using ingredients that are both safe to eat as well as healthy and nutritious. And the recipes in this book are designed to help. They are plant-based choices that are characteristically high in whole grains, rich in fiber, and low in calories. In addition to being allergen-free, they are also free of gluten and refined white sugar. As an added bonus, they are satisfying and delicious.

Eating healthy meals and snacks is especially important for children because good habits that begin at a young age are likely to carry through to adulthood. Whether you have food allergies or not, healthy eating offers undeniable benefits. It helps maintain a healthy weight, increases energy, and reduces the chance of getting sick. Let's take a closer look at these benefits.

Encourages Good Eating Habits

Are you familiar with the term "mindless eating"? If you've ever found yourself munching away while sitting in front of the TV or a computer screen without even realizing that you're eating, let alone *how much* you are eating; if your hand has a tendency to keep plunging into that snack bowl and then make its way to your mouth with no thought involved, then you have experienced mindless eating firsthand.

Unfortunately, we have become a nation of mindless eaters who eat out of boredom, to be social, or simply because the food is in front of us. These poor eating habits coupled with lack of exercise and unhealthy food choices play an undeniable role in the country's growing obesity problem, which currently affects nearly 30 percent of adults over the age of twenty, and around 17 percent of children and adolescents between ages two and nineteen.

Instead of eating simply for the sake of eating, take time to think before you eat. Be aware of when, what, and how much you're eating. This

DOGGONE FOODS!

Did you know that even our furry friends can be allergic to certain foods? Soy, wheat gluten, dairy, fish, beef, and lamb are among the biggest offenders for both cats and dogs—and itchy skin rashes are the usual symptoms. Interestingly, these foods are also the most common products found in commercial pet foods. The good news is that hypoallergenic food is available.

In addition to foods that cause allergies, a number of foods can actually be toxic to animals like cats and dogs and make them seriously ill. Never give the following to your furry friends:

❏ **AVOCADO.** The skin, fruit, and pit of avocados are toxic and can cause gastrointestinal and respiratory problems.

❏ **CHOCOLATE.** Chocolate contains a stimulant that can affect heart rate and the central nervous system.

❏ **FRUIT PITS/SEEDS.** The pits and seeds of many fruits, such as apples, pears, peaches, and cherries, contain poisonous cyanide. When ingested, serious respiratory problems or even death can result; they can also become lodged in the intestinal tract.

❏ **GRAPES, RAISINS, CURRANTS.** These fruits contain a toxin that can cause kidney damage.

❏ **MACADAMIA NUTS/WALNUTS.** Nuts in general are not good for pets; but these two varieties can affect the heart, muscles, and the nervous and digestive systems.

❏ **MILK/DAIRY PRODUCTS.** Dairy products contain lactose, which may cause diarrhea and other digestive issues.

❏ **ONIONS/GARLIC.** Both onions and garlic contain sulfoxides and disulfides, which can damage red blood cells and cause anemia, especially in cats.

❏ **SALT.** Sodium can lead to a number of serious problems including kidney failure and neurological conditions like seizures and coma.

❏ **XYLITOL.** This sweetener, found in many sugar-free candies, chewing gums, breath mints, and baked goods can cause liver failure.

❏ **YEAST DOUGH.** When it is ingested, yeast dough can expand in the digestive system and cause pain, bloating, and a possible rupture.

awareness will help you and your family become "mindful" eaters.

Increases Energy

Because the recipes in this book are filled with fiber-rich complex carbohydrates—whole grains, fruits, and vegetables—they provide fuel for the body. Complex carbohydrates, which are digested slowly, will help you feel satisfied for long periods after eating. They also help stabilize blood sugar and maintain even energy levels. We call them "upper foods."

On the other hand, we avoid simple carbohydrates, such as white sugar, white flour, and any products that contain them. These refined, processed "downer foods," contain very little if any fiber, which means they are digested quickly. This causes blood sugar levels to spike quickly and then drop dramatically—in other words the body initially feels a quick burst of energy that is soon followed by a noticeable energy drop. Simple carbs are also linked to cravings, compulsive eating, and irritability.

Characteristically rich in fiber, the choices in this book will help curb those hunger pangs and provide the needed energy to get through any slumps during the day.

Promotes Good Health

Along with being fiber-rich, the choices in this book are packed with vitamins and minerals for increased nutritional value. And as an added benefit, they don't contain artery-clogging saturated fats.

Saturated fats contribute to high levels of *low-density lipoproteins* (LDLs) or bad cholesterol, a leading risk factor in coronary heart disease, diabetes, and stroke. A recent issue of *Annals of Internal Medicine* published the results of a study that examined the link between bad cholesterol levels in young adults and the development of heart disease later on. Under the guidance of Dr. Mark J. Pletcher, researchers at the University of California, San Francisco, analyzed data from 3,528 men and women who had been tracked for twenty years by the CARDIA study (Coronary Artery Risk Development in Young Adults). At the beginning of the study, the age of the participants ranged from eighteen to thirty years old. The researchers found that the participants with histories of high LDL levels as young adults were five and a half times more likely to have a buildup of calcium in their coronary arteries than those with low LDL levels.

The fats in our recipes come from heart-healthy foods like avocados and oils such as olive, sunflower, and grapeseed. These fats help raise the *high-density lipoproteins* (HDLs), also known as good cholesterol. HDLs help rid the body of LDLs and reduce the risk of heart disease and stroke. A growing amount of evidence also shows that HDLs may even offer extra protection against certain cancers.

SUMMING IT UP

The only way to prevent an allergic food reaction is to avoid the problem food. But avoidance does not mean you have to feel deprived. It doesn't mean a limited diet of bland, unappealing meals and snacks—and the delicious choices found in this book will prove it.

2

Stocking the Kitchen

If you, your children, or other family members have food allergies, it's a good idea to keep a variety of kitchen staples on hand. Having the right ingredients will make it easy for you to prepare healthy, allergen-free meals and snacks, including the recipes in this book, at any time.

In the last chapter, we talked about the foods and ingredients *to avoid.* This chapter is all about the best ones *to choose.* One of our strongest recommendations is to select foods that are as close to their natural state as possible. This means whole foods, including fresh fruits and vegetables, whole grains, and beans that preferably are locally grown. It also means using unrefined natural sweeteners like honey, fruit juice, date sugar, and maple syrup. Whole foods and whole food products are not processed (or are minimally processed) so they are close to their natural, nutrient-rich state. And organically grown foods and the products made from them are the best.

WHY ORGANIC?

Organic foods are grown in rich soil that is free of pesticides and synthetic fertilizers. They do not contain chemical additives, hormones, or preservatives. And since they are very close to their natural state, they taste better, too.

Another important reason to choose organic —especially for those with allergies—is that it means avoiding *genetically modified food* (GM food), which comes from *genetically modified organisms* (GMOs). Simply put, the genes of GM plants have been altered or artificially manipulated to mix and match the DNA of totally different species, often for the purpose of growing a bigger, better version of the crop or to create one that is resistant to pesticides and herbicides. The genetically modified Flavr Savr Tomato, for example, was spliced with a gene that prevented the breakdown of its cell walls, resulting in a firmer tomato with a longer shelf life.

Nearly 80 percent of the corn and over 90 percent of the soybeans grown in the United States are genetically modified. The most popular herbicide-resistant GM crops are Monsanto Company's Roundup Ready crops, which are engineered to be resistant to Monsanto's own broad spectrum herbicide called Roundup. Because the plants are resistant to the herbicide, growers are able to douse their fields with it, killing the weeds and pests without harming the crops themselves. Growers no longer need to till the soil to control weeds.

While there have been many arguments in favor of genetically modified foods, there are a growing number of reasons against them. Concerns for the environment and human health are the most obvious. And those with allergies need to be especially concerned. One of the biggest fears is that splicing genes between two different species can inadvertently incorporate an allergenic protein into the modified crop or cause the formation of a new one. Cross-pollination is another concern. An increasing number of researchers are finding links between the consumption of GM crops and the creation or worsening of food allergies

Organic foods do not contain genetically modified ingredients, so it is best to choose them whenever possible. This is especially recommended when buying soybeans and corn (the most common GM crops) and any products that contain them.

"9 IS FINE"

Another way to avoid genetically modified produce is by checking the Price Look-Up (PLU) code, which is found on a tiny label that is stuck on the fruit or vegetable. The PLU code for GM produce has five numbers that begin with the number 8. Organically grown fruits and vegetables have five numbers that begin with the number 9. The PLU code for non-GM produce that is grown through conventional farming methods (which likely means the use of pesticides, herbicides, and/or chemical fertilizers) has only four numbers. An easy way to remember organic varieties is by keeping in mind that "9 is fine."

WHERE TO SHOP

Fortunately, due to an increasing demand for whole and organic foods, when it comes to shopping, you have a number of good options.

Farmers' markets that sell fresh organic produce are located in towns and cities throughout the United States. Buying from local farmers means getting freshly picked fruits and vegetables—and the fresher the produce, the greater its nutritional value. As soon as that apple is picked, its vitamin and mineral content begins to diminish. Most of the produce found on supermarket shelves was picked four to seven days earlier and transported an average of 1,500 miles. Local farmers' markets assure fresher foods than what you'll find in the supermarket, and you will be supporting local growers. To locate a farmers' market in your area, visit the following website for a national map of market locations: *www.ams.usda.gov/farmersmarkets/map.htm*

Natural foods markets also sell whole foods like fruits, vegetables, whole grains, and whole grain products that are typically organic. Many of the larger stores offer extensive selections, and their product turnover rate is usually quick, which is a good indication of freshness. Although natural foods markets are more expensive than most other stores, they tend to support local farmers and sustainable agricultural practices.

A growing number of supermarkets are beginning to carry whole foods and organic products. They are conveniently located, which is a plus; however, their selection is often limited and product turnover may be slow, which could mean compromised freshness.

Finally, you can also purchase organic foods online. We have bought a number of grains and grain products from reputable online companies, and have included a list of those responsible suppliers in the Resources beginning on page 174.

Another thing to keep in mind when buying organic is that packaged foods often contain multiple ingredients. The word "organic" appearing on a label does not necessarily mean that the product is 100-percent organic. (See the inset on "Organic Product Labeling" below.)

ALLERGEN-FREE KITCHEN MUST HAVES

The following list of allergen-free foods and ingredients is certainly not complete, but it does include the products we recommend to keep handy in your kitchen. (Many are used in our recipes.) The products you choose will depend, of course, on the particular type of food allergy you are dealing with. When buying packaged items, always check ingredients labels carefully, even those products you have bought before—manufacturers often change product ingredients without warning. A list of recommended product brands and companies that sell allergen-free foods is found in the Resources beginning on page 174.

ORGANIC PRODUCT LABELING

Understanding organic labeling can be a little confusing, especially for products that contain more than one ingredient. In an effort to help consumers understand the organic content of the food they buy, the USDA has established the following labeling rules:

SINGLE-INGREDIENT FOODS

For fruits, vegetables, and other single-ingredient foods, a sticker version of the USDA Organic seal (above) may appear on the products themselves or on a sign above them.

MULTI-INGREDIENT FOODS

For packaged foods that contain more than one ingredient, the following labeling terms are used to indicate their organic content:

❑ **100% ORGANIC.** The product must contain 100% organic ingredients. It is permitted to use the USDA seal.

❑ **ORGANIC.** The product must contain 95 to 100% organic ingredients. It is permitted to use the USDA seal.

❑ **MADE WITH ORGANIC INGREDIENTS.** The product must contain at least 70% organic ingredients.

❑ **CONTAINS ORGANIC INGREDIENTS.** The product contains less than 70% organic ingredients.

It is also important to know that even if a producer is certified organic, using the USDA Organic seal is voluntary. In addition, the process of becoming certified is very demanding, and not all producers of organic foods are willing to go through it, especially small farming operations. For this reason, never hesitate to ask vendors, such as those at farmers' markets, how their products are grown.

Milk Substitutes

Rice milk (light and mild flavored), oat milk (mild flavored), and hemp milk (rich and nutty flavored). For optimal nutrition, choose organic varieties that are fortified with calcium and vitamins D, B, and E. Coconut milk is another alternative. Thick and rich, it makes an especially good substitute for cream. If nuts are not a concern, blending one part cashews with one part water results in another good cream alternative.

Egg Substitutes

Ener-G Egg Replacer (for baking only). To make your own egg-free substitute for baking pur-

FACTS ON FATS

FRIEND FATS

According to the American Heart Association, a heart-healthy diet can contain up to 30 percent of calories from fat, provided that most of the fat is unsaturated. Unsaturated fats, which include monounsaturated and polyunsaturated varieties, are "friendly fats" that lower harmful LDL cholesterol levels. Monounsaturated fats are found in olive oil and canola oil. Polyunsaturated fats are found in corn, flax, grapeseed, safflower, sesame, and sunflower oils

FOE FATS

Saturated fats are not your friends! They increase LDL cholesterol (the bad cholesterol), which clogs arteries and can lead to heart disease. Saturated fat, found mainly in animal sources like whole milk, butter, and fatty meats, has also been linked to an increased risk of type-2 diabetes.

Another "foe" to avoid is hydrogenated fat. This type of fat is created when hydrogen is added to an oil (often unsaturated) to make it solid at room temperature. During this process, the fat becomes more saturated. Trans fats, con-

sidered the worst of the saturated fats, are created during the processing of foods through partial hydrogenation. Trans fats are often found in commercial products such as crackers, snack chips, baked goods, and frozen items like waffles and French fries.

RECIPE CHOICES

We use "heart healthy" fats in our recipes, such as those found in cold-pressed virgin and extra-virgin olive oils and grapeseed oil (organic, of course). The beneficial essential fatty acids they contain are also critical for nerve and brain functioning. Unfortunately, many commercial varieties of these oils are subjected to chemical and heat processing that causes the formation of harmful free radicals. This is why we advocate using organic, cold-pressed, minimally processed oils. We also recommend storing the oil in a dark glass container and keeping it in the refrigerator to prevent rancidity.

As for using other oils, we avoid nut oils—for obvious reasons—and do not advocate the use of corn oil, which, unless it is organic, is likely to contain GMOs. We also avoid canola oil because of the controversy regarding its safety.

poses, try any of the following ingredient combinations, each of which is equivalent to one egg:

❏ 1 tablespoon flaxseed or chia seed meal plus 3 tablespoons warm water. Let sit three minutes.

❏ 1 teaspoon baking powder plus 1 tablespoon apple cider vinegar.

❏ 1 tablespoon agar plus 1 tablespoon water.

Grains and Flours

The following grains and the flours/meals made from them are gluten free: amaranth, buckwheat, chickpeas, corn, millet, oats, quinoa, rice, sorghum, and teff. Also acceptable are the following flours (not from grains): lentil flour, potato flour, and tapioca flour. For a basic gluten-free baking mix, see the recipe on page 151.

Be aware that oats and oat flour are often processed in facilities that also handle wheat (and other gluten-containing grains like rye and barley), so cross-contamination may occur. Make sure to purchase varieties that are certified wheat- or gluten-free.

Seeds and Seed Butters

Flaxseeds, flaxseed meal, pumpkin seeds, sesame seeds, sunflower butter, and tahini (sesame seed butter). Please note if you are allergic to tree nuts, all of these seeds (with the exception of sesame seeds) are rarely allergenic and considered acceptable. Be aware, however, that although sesame seeds are not on the current list of top allergens by the FDA, reactions to them—often serious—are on the rise.

Also be aware that some seed butters are processed in facilities that also manufacture nut butters, so cross-contamination may occur. If necessary, contact the manufacturer to verify that the product is nut free.

Oils

Grapeseed, safflower, sunflower, sesame, coconut, and extra-virgin olive oil.

Baking Products and Thickeners

Baking powder (aluminum- and albumin-free), baking soda, arrowroot, tapioca flour, agar powder, and potato starch. Also make sure baking powder does not contain lecithin, which could be derived from a soy or egg source.

Breads and Bread Products

Gluten-free/allergen-free varieties of bread and bread crumbs, bagels, buns, muffins, pitas, rolls, brown rice tortillas, and corn tortillas. Keep in mind that brown rice tortillas are fairly stiff—they are good for quesadillas, but they do not make good wrappers for foods like burritos or taquitos, which need to be rolled up.

Cereals (dry, ready to eat)

Gluten free/allergen-free varieties, such as amaranth flakes, corn flakes, flax flakes, oat circles, puffed millet, puffed corn, and puffed rice.

Fresh Fruits (preferably organic)

Apples, peaches, pears, bananas, etc, and citrus fruits (lemons, oranges, grapefruits, tangerines, mandarins, clementines).

Fresh Vegetables (preferably organic)

Vegetables such as avocados, broccoli, cabbage, carrots, cauliflower, corn (organic only), cucumbers, eggplant, garlic, lettuce, mushrooms, onions, peas, potatoes, scallions, spinach, squash, sweet potatoes, tomatoes, and yams.

Sweeteners (preferably organic)

Agave nectar, coconut sugar, date sugar, fruit juice (orange, apple), fruit concentrate (frozen), fruit syrup, honey, pure maple syrup, and rice syrup.

Canned and Bottled Goods

Beans (black beans, chickpeas, kidney beans, etc.), corn (organic only), fruit-sweetened jams, olives, pumpkin purée, and tomato sauce.

Snack Foods and Frozen Desserts

Raisins and other dried fruit (unsulfured); unsweetened fruit strips or roll ups. Gluten-free/allergen-free products like corn chips, flax crackers, oat crackers, popcorn, rice cakes, and rice crackers. Frozen items such as sorbets, frozen fruit, fruit juice ice pops, and Rice Dream brand frozen treats.

Pasta and Noodles

Brown rice pasta, corn pasta, quinoa pasta, buckwheat noodles, Papadini lentil/bean pasta, and rice noodles (rice sticks).

Seasonings and Flavor Enhancers

Apple cider vinegar, balsamic vinegar, black pepper, carob powder, cinnamon, coconut aminos (see page 145), fresh/dried herbs (basil, rosemary, thyme, cilantro, oregano), garlic powder, garlic salt, ketchup, lemons, limes, mustard, nutmeg, nutritional yeast (see page 117), onion powder, pickles, salsa, sea salt, Tabasco or other hot sauce, and pure vanilla extract.

Once again, all of the foods and products listed above are safe for those who are allergic to any of the top eight food allergens—peanuts, tree nuts, milk, eggs, wheat, soy, fish, and crustacean shellfish. They are also gluten-free, making them acceptable choices for those with celiac disease. It isn't necessary to stock *all* of the recommended ingredients listed, as your choices will depend on the specific allergenic foods you need to avoid.

RECIPE ADJUSTING

When you are cooking for someone with food allergies, you will undoubtedly find yourself on a constant search for "safe" foods and recipes that are allergen-fee. The good news is that due to the growing number of people with food allergies, there is also a growing number of available recipes and meal ideas. Whether it is through books, magazines, or Internet sites, you can find plenty of recipes that cater either to one specific food allergen or many.

Although it is helpful (and certainly convenient) that so many allergy-specific recipes exist, it can be just as helpful to know how to adapt those recipes that are not allergen-free. By knowing how to replace allergenic ingredients with safe substitutions, you can make new (often improved) versions of those family favorite holiday cookies or that delicious-sounding muffin recipe you came across in a magazine.

Knowing how to adapt and adjust is a skill that often takes just a little guidance, patience, and experience. To help you out, we have created the chart "Ingredient Substitutions for Recipe

HERBS: FRESH OR DRIED?

When it comes to using herbs and spices, we recommend fresh when possible. If using dried, be sure to check expiration dates. Most dried herbs lose their potency within a few months.

I tablespoon fresh = I teaspoon dried

Adjustments" on pages 28 and 29. In it we have listed some of the most common allergenic ingredients found in recipes along with some suggested ingredient substitutions.

SOME HELPFUL TIPS

Before you start making the delicious dishes in the following chapters, we'd like to share a few quick tips and guidelines with you. Hopefully, you will find them helpful when preparing the recipes.

❏ In most recipes, honey is our liquid sweetener of choice; however, feel free to use equal amounts of pure maple syrup, agave nectar, rice syrup, or another natural liquid sweetener instead.

❏ Honey can sometimes crystallize. If this happens, place it in a heat-resistant glass cup or container and set it in a pan or bowl of hot water. As it begins to heat up, stir the honey until it returns to a smooth liquid state.

❏ If a recipe calls for oil and a liquid sweetener, first measure the oil. After emptying out the oil, use the same measuring cup (don't clean it) to measure the sweetener. The oil residue on the cup will allow the sticky sweetener to slide out easily.

❏ For even baking, unless otherwise instructed in a recipe, bake the food on the center oven rack.

❏ To get the most juice out of fresh lemons, limes, or oranges, roll them against the kitchen countertop before squeezing.

❏ When using oat flour, make sure it is certified pure oat flour with no possible presence of wheat or gluten.

❏ We use primarily nondairy rice and oat milk in our recipes. If soy or tree nuts are not a concern, you can use soy and/or almond milk instead.

❏ For the sake of time, we use canned beans in our recipes. We recommend organic varieties that are free of salt.

Fruit and Veggie Wash

Always wash your fruits and vegetables before eating. Even organic varieties are likely to contain bacteria from processing, shipping, and handling. Here's the simple recipe we use and recommend:

1. Place the ingredients in a spray bottle and shake well.

2. Spray the fruit/veggies with the wash, scrub gently with your hands, then rinse with cold water.

3. Store any remaining wash in the refrigerator.

1 cup water

2 tablespoons fresh lemon juice, vinegar, salt, or baking soda

Ingredient Substitutions for Recipe Adjustments

When adjusting the ingredients in a recipe to suit specific allergenic needs, you may find the following substitution chart helpful. It offers some suggested ingredient options for a number of common food allergens. Be aware that these substitutions do not include any of the eight major food allergens. Also be aware that, depending on the specific allergy, you can expand these options. For instance, if you need to avoid dairy but not soy, you can include soymilk as a milk option.

ALLERGENIC FOOD	SUGGESTED SUBSTITUTIONS	BEST USES
Cocoa	Carob powder in equal measure.	As a flavor-enhancer in smoothies and other beverages, desserts, and baked goods.
Cow's milk	Rice milk, hemp milk, oat milk, or coconut milk in equal measure.	As an ingredient in baked goods, smoothies, and light cream-style soups and sauces.
Buttermilk	Mix 1 tablespoon lemon juice or apple cider vinegar with 1 cup of the milks listed above. Let sit a few minutes to thicken.	As an ingredient in baked goods and cream-style sauces.
Cream	Potato purée in equal measure.	As a thickener in soups and sauces.
Egg (1 large)	Mix 1 tablespoon flaxseed or chia seed meal with 3 tablespoons warm water. Let sit a few minutes to thicken.	As a binder in baked goods.
	$1/4$ cup applesauce or puréed fruit.*	As a binder in baked goods. Also adds moisture.

ALLERGENIC FOOD	SUGGESTED SUBSTITUTIONS	BEST USES
Egg (1 large)	Mix 1 tablespoon agar powder with 1 tablespoon water.	As a binder in baked goods.
	Mix 2 teaspoons baking powder with 2 tablespoons water and 1 tablespoon vegetable oil.	As a leavening agent in baked goods.
	Ener-G Egg Replacer (prepare as directed on package).	As a leavening agent in baked goods.
Peanut butter / Nut butters	Sunflower seed butter and sesame seed butter (tahini) in equal measure.	As an ingredient in baked goods, desserts, and smoothies.
Wheat flour (1 cup)**	$3/4$ cup brown rice flour, $3/4$ cup potato flour, $3/4$ cup chickpea flour, 1 cup tapioca or arrowroot flour, or $1^1/4$ cups oat flour *Suggested Flour Combination:* $2/3$ cup rice flour + $1/4$ cup potato flour + 2 tablespoons tapioca or arrowroot flour	As an ingredient in baked goods, and as a thickener in soups and sauces.
White sugar (1 cup)†	$3/4$ cup agave nectar, $3/4$ cup date sugar $3/4$ cup honey $3/4$ cup maple syrup $3/4$ cup rice syrup	As an ingredient in baked goods, desserts, and smoothies.

*When using puréed fruit, baked goods tend to come out a little heavy and dense. For this reason, adding an additional $1/2$ teaspoon baking powder to the recipe is recommended.

**When making flour substitutions for baked goods, don't expect to achieve the same texture and consistency as with wheat flour. For best results, experimenting may be necessary, depending on the particular recipe.

† Although white sugar is not an allergenic food, it is included in this table because it is a common ingredient in many recipes and not a healthy choice.

❏ Our recipes generally call for oat flour and brown rice flour; however, amaranth, buckwheat, chickpea, millet, potato, quinoa, and teff flours can be substituted in equal amounts.

Many of the recipes in this book, especially the snacks, can be made in advance and stored in the refrigerator or freezer. Having prepared food on hand is especially convenient for satisfying those hunger attacks at a moment's notice.

HAPPY EATING!

Now that you are armed with the information you need to prepare healthful, allergen-free dishes, it's time to get started. Keep in mind that having dietary restrictions doesn't mean deprivation. Rather, it is an opportunity to be more creative with food. And making your own meals and snacks lets you monitor the ingredients to guarantee safe eating.

IMPORTANT WORD ABOUT THE RECIPES

The dishes in this book are made without eggs, cow's milk or other dairy products, soy, wheat (or other grains containing gluten), peanuts, tree nuts, fish, or shellfish—the most common allergenic foods according to the current assessment of the U.S. Food and Drug Administration.

Of course, most people with food allergies are allergic to one, maybe even a few of these ingredients—but not to all of them. For this reason, keep in mind that you can prepare the recipes in this book as written or alter the ingredients to suit individual dietary needs. For instance, if nut allergies are not a problem, feel free to add some chopped walnuts to a cookie recipe or sprinkle them over a fresh green salad for added crunch. Try using almond butter instead of sunflower butter in Mrs. Marple's Maple Meltaways, or add a spoonful of peanut butter to the Carob-Banana Smoothie. If dairy foods are not allergenic, top your pizza with some shredded mozzarella or a sprinkling of Parmesan. You get the idea.

The person you are cooking for may also be allergic to an ingredient in a recipe that is not considered one of the major food allergens—ingredients such as tomatoes, onions, peaches, and sesame seeds to name a few. You can either prepare the recipe without the problem ingredient or try using a substitute. Simply put, you can serve the dishes in this book as they are or use them as springboards for creating any number of delicious variations. Most important, no matter what you choose to do, no matter how you decide to alter the recipes, you can feel good in knowing that they are not only allergen-free, but healthy as well. Enjoy!

3

Drinkable Delights

Whether you're looking for a refreshing thirst quencher or trying to satisfy a midday hunger crave, you've come to the right place. The following pages are filled with bright, delicious, healthful drinks—liquid refreshments ranging from thick, rich smoothies and fruity juice drinks to herbal iced teas and fizzy delights. And because they are made with fresh, nutritious ingredients, you can feel good about serving them.

We believe just about everyone enjoys smoothies. In addition to making satisfying snacks, they can be served as light breakfasts, simple desserts, or accompaniments to just about any meal. The basic foundation of any smoothie is fruit or fruit juice that is blended with ice, which adds frosty thickness. But there are lots of other ingredients that can transform the simplest smoothie into a luscious beverage with added flavor and nutrition. The "Create-a Smoothie" inset on page 34 presents an extensive list of suggested ingredients for making delicious drinks that are rich sources of vitamins, minerals, and other healthful nutrients.

Along with ice, many smoothies—especially those sold at your local food court—contain soy or dairy products as thickeners. Our allergy-free smoothies are thickened with ingredients like bananas, fruit sorbet, sunflower seed butter, and even avocados and rolled oats—all with rich, delicious results.

So take out the blender and get ready to wow your family with some of our favorite drinkable delights. From the luscious Banana Cream Pie Smoothie to the refreshing Mixed-Berry Blast to the exotic Hibiscus Pomegranate Iced Tea—all of the choices are easy to make, fun to drink, and good for you! What could be better?

Oatmeal-Apple Pie Smoothie

Fiber-rich oats add creamy thickness to this smoothie,
which tastes a lot like apple pie.

Yield: 2 servings
(about 8 ounces each)

. . . .

1/4 cup rolled oats

1 cup apple juice

2 large sweet apples,
peeled and diced

1 teaspoon ground
cinnamon

8 ice cubes

1. Place the oats and apple juice in a blender and let soak for 2 to 3 minutes.

2. Add all of the remaining ingredients, and blend on high speed until the mixture is smooth and the ice is well crushed.

3. Serve immediately. (Be aware that this smoothie will get thicker the longer it sits. If you don't drink it right away, you may have to add more apple juice.)

CHANGE IT UP . . .

- For an even creamier texture and added flavor, include 1 tablespoon sunflower butter or 2 tablespoons soaked raw sunflower seeds in Step 2.

- Try substituting coconut milk for the apple juice.

FROZEN FRUIT OR ICE CUBES?

The foundation of any smoothie is fruit or fruit juice that is often thickened with ice. Instead of ice, you can use frozen fruit. Either buy fruit that is already frozen or freeze your own fresh varieties. Wash the fruit, dry it well, and then place it in a zip-lock freezer bag. This is an especially good idea for berries, which are not always in season and spoil quickly. Frozen, they can last for months!

Banana Cream Pie Smoothie

*This smoothie is really rich and delicious.
If you use fresh (not frozen) bananas,
add another 2 or 3 ice cubes.*

1. Place all of the ingredients in a blender.

2. Blend on high speed until the mixture is smooth and the ice is well crushed.

3. Serve immediately.

Yield: 2 servings
(about 8 ounces each)
. . . .
2 large frozen bananas, sliced

1 1/2 cups coconut milk

1 1/2 cups rice milk

2 tablespoons pure maple syrup

1 tablespoon toasted sunflower seeds (optional)

1 teaspoon vanilla

1/4 teaspoon ground nutmeg

6 ice cubes

Berry Coconut Smoothie

Very "coco nutty" and berry berry good!

1. Place all of the ingredients in a blender.

2. Blend on high speed until the mixture is smooth and the ice is well crushed.

3. Serve immediately.

Yield: 2 servings
(about 8 ounces each)
. . . .
1 cup frozen strawberries

1 cup frozen blueberries

1 cup vanilla-flavored coconut yogurt

3/4 cup water

6 ice cubes

CREATE-A-SMOOTHIE!

Smoothies are healthy, satisfying ways to enjoy fruit! And you can whip one up in a matter of minutes! Although the foundation of a basic smoothie is fruit or fruit juice that is often thickened with ice, there are lots of ingredients (and ingredient combinations) that can turn a simple smoothie into a luscious drink with added flavor, richness, and nutritional value. We've listed some of our favorite smoothie ingredients below. Have fun coming up with your own flavorful creations!

JUICES

- Acai
- Apple
- Blueberry
- Carrot
- Cherry
- Cranberry
- Goji berry
- Grape
- Grapefruit
- Kiwi
- Mango
- Orange
- Papaya
- Peach
- Pear
- Pineapple
- Pomegranate
- Raspberry
- Strawberry
- Watermelon

WHOLE FRUITS (PEELED/PITTED)

- Apricots
- Bananas
- Blackberries
- Blueberries
- Cantaloupes
- Grapes
- Honeydews
- Kiwis
- Mangoes
- Papayas
- Peaches
- Pears
- Plums
- Raspberries
- Strawberries
- Watermelon

THICKENERS

- Avocados
- Bananas
- Ice cubes
- Rolled oats, soaked
- Sorbet
- Sunflower butter
- Sunflower seeds, soaked
- Tahini

FLAVORFUL GOODIES

- Acai berries/purée
- Agave nectar
- Brown rice syrup
- Carob powder
- Cinnamon
- Coconut flakes
- Coconut milk
- Dates
- Ginger*
- Goji berries
- Honey
- Lemon/lime juice
- Maple syrup
- Rice milk
- Seed butters
- Seeds (chia, hemp, sunflower)
- Tea
- Vanilla extract

* Fresh ginger is very strong. Start with just a little—a scant 1/4 teaspoon of grated ginger per 12-ounce drink—then adjust as desired.

Blueberry-Banana Green Tea Smoothie

This combination of green tea and blueberries is not only delicious, but also supplies a healthy dose of antioxidants.

1. Place all of the ingredients in a blender.

2. Blend on high speed until the mixture is smooth and the ice is well crushed.

3. Serve immediately.

CHANGE IT UP . . .

- Use raspberries or strawberries instead of blueberries, or try any berry combination.

Yield: 4 servings
(about 8 ounces each)

2 cups green tea, steeped and chilled

2 cups frozen blueberries

2 large frozen bananas, cut into small chunks

1 tablespoon toasted sunflower seeds (optional)

6 ice cubes

Grape-Raspberry Smoothie

Frosty and refreshing!

1. Place all of the ingredients in a blender.

2. Blend on high speed until the mixture is smooth and the ice is well crushed.

3. Serve immediately.

Yield: 2 servings
(about 8 ounces each)

1 1/2 cups frozen raspberries

1 1/2 cups grape juice

1 teaspoon vanilla

6 ice cubes

Honeydew Kiwi Sensation

Super refreshing!

Yield: 2 servings
(about 8 ounces each)

• • • • • • • •

2 cups cubed honeydew

1 1/2 cups cubed kiwi

1 tablespoon lime juice

1 tablespoon honey

2 fresh mint leaves

1 teaspoon vanilla

6 to 8 ice cubes

1. Place all of the ingredients in a blender.

2. Blend on high speed until the mixture is smooth and the ice is well crushed.

3. Serve immediately.

Strawberry-Apple Green Smoothie

Apples and strawberries add sweet goodness to this nutrient-rich drink.

Yield: 2 servings
(about 8 ounces each)

• • • • • • • •

1 cup chopped baby spinach leaves

1 cup frozen strawberries

1 medium apple, peeled and cut into small chunks

3/4 cup apple juice

8 ice cubes

1. Place all of the ingredients in a blender.

2. Blend on high speed until the ice is well crushed and the mixture is well blended and a bit pulpy.

3. Serve immediately.

CHANGE IT UP . . .

• Instead of spinach, try using chopped fresh kale.

Orange Granola Smoothie

Crunchy granola adds wonderful texture to this smoothie.

1. Place all of the ingredients in a blender.

2. Blend on high speed until the mixture is well blended and the ice is well crushed.

3. Serve immediately.

Yield: 2 servings
(about 8 ounces each)

. . . .

1 3/4 cups orange juice

3/4 cup Great Gluten-Free Granola (page 165)

2 large frozen banana, sliced

1 tablespoon honey or pure maple syrup

6 ice cubes

Hibiscus Pomegranate Iced Tea

Fruity and a little tart, this refreshing iced tea is a summertime favorite.

1. Add the tea to the boiling water. Remove from the heat and let steep at least 5 to 10 minutes. (Steep longer for stronger flavor.)

2. Strain the tea (or remove the tea bags) and pour into a large pitcher. Stir in the pomegranate juice, vanilla, and cold water.

3. Refrigerate at least 2 hours or until chilled.

CHANGE IT UP . . .

- Try this tea with different juices. Grape, mango, and blueberry are great choices.

Yield: 6 servings
(about 12 ounces each)

. . . .

1/4 cup loose hibiscus tea, or 12 tea bags

4 cups boiling water

1 cup pomegranate juice

1/2 teaspoon vanilla

4 cups cold water

Mixed-Berry Blast

Acai berries add mildly sweet, slightly tart flavor to the other berries in this drink.

Yield: 2 servings
(about 8 ounces each)

$1/2$ cup fresh blackberries

$1/2$ cup fresh blueberries

$1/2$ cup fresh raspberries

4 tablespoons frozen acai purée

$1/2$ cup pomegranate juice

2 tablespoons toasted flaxseeds (optional)

1 tablespoon honey or pure maple syrup (optional)

8 ice cubes

1. Place all of the ingredients in a blender.

2. Blend on high speed until the mixture is smooth and the ice is well crushed.

3. Serve immediately.

Iced Mint Green Tea

Fresh mint gives this iced tea a refreshing boost.

Yield: 4 servings
(about 8 ounces each)

4 green tea bags

$1/2$ cup fresh mint leaves

$2 1/2$ tablespoons honey

1 tablespoon lemon juice

4 cups boiling water

1. Add all of the ingredients to the boiling water. Remove from the heat and let steep for 8 to 10 minutes. (Steep longer for stronger flavor.) Transfer to a pitcher.

2. Refrigerate at least 2 hours before serving.

Carob-Banana Smoothie

*Carob gives this frosty smoothie
its chocolaty flavor.*

1. Dissolve the carob in 2 tablespoons of the rice milk, then transfer to a blender along with the remaining ingredients.

2. Blend on high speed until the mixture is smooth and the ice is well crushed.

3. Serve immediately.

Yield: 2 servings
(about 8 ounces each)

1 $^3/_4$ cups rice milk

2 tablespoons carob powder

2 medium-sized bananas, cut into small chunks

5 dates, pitted and chopped

1 tablespoon toasted sunflower seeds (optional)

6 ice cubes

Pineapple-Watermelon Fizz

*Sparkling water provides a burst of bubbles
in this thirst-quenching drink.*

1. Add the pineapple juice and watermelon to a blender or food processor, and blend until smooth.

2. Transfer the mixture to a pitcher, add the sparkling water, and gently stir.

3. Serve over ice.

Yield: 4 servings
(about 8 ounces each)

6-ounce can frozen pineapple juice concentrate

4 cups cubed watermelon

1 cup sparkling water

Tropical Delight

*Serve this fruity island special as is or garnished
with a wedge of fresh pineapple.*

Yield: 2 servings
(about 8 ounces each)

1 cup diced frozen
pineapple

2 cups diced frozen
mango or papaya

1 cup orange juice

1/2 teaspoon vanilla

6 ice cubes

1. Place all of the ingredients in a blender.
2. Blend on high speed until the mixture is smooth and the ice is well crushed.
3. Serve immediately.

CHANGE IT UP ...

- For added flavor and creamy texture, add a frozen banana to this drink.
- Substitute pineapple juice or coconut milk for the orange juice.

4

Chips, Dips 'n Savory Snacks

Want to see a disappearing act? It's easy. Simply surround a bowl of fresh salsa with crisp corn chips, or set out a basket of pita crisps alongside some creamy hummus, and then stand back and watch it vanish! When it comes to snacks, pairing crunchy chips with flavorful dips is always a hit. The good news is that everyone—even those with food allergies—can enjoy these popular treats. And in this chapter, you'll find a delectable assortment of salsas, spreads, and yummy dips, as well as crunchy crisps, crackers, and chips to go with them.

We have included appetizing classics like Easy Guacamole, Super Salsa, and a number of hummus varieties, as well as many of our personal favorites, including a fiery Jalapeño Bean Dip, a lemon-kissed Chunky Corn Relish, and a silky smooth Velvety White Bean Dip. In addition to being scooped up by chips, crackers, or fresh raw vegetables, many of these dips and spreads can be added to your favorite sandwich, spooned over a steaming hot baked potato, or used to garnish a fresh green salad. Talk about versatile!

If you want to try your hand at making your own chips and crackers, you'll find plenty of choices on the following pages, including Light 'n Flaky Oat Crisps, Brown Rice Chia Crisps, and Crunchy Croutons. The recipes for Baked Tortilla Chips and Krispy Kale Chips are so easy to make, you'll find yourself choosing them over commercial brands every time!

Along with the recipes, we have included some helpful food preparation guidelines, such as how to roast bell peppers and hydrate sun-dried tomatoes. We've also shown you how to roast a head of garlic, and then use the melt-in-your-mouth cloves as a heavenly spread.

It doesn't matter which dips, spreads, or chips you select from this chapter, or how you decide to serve them. They are all simple to prepare, versatile, and really tasty. Just don't expect to have any leftovers!

Super Salsa

Yield: About 3 1/2 cups

- I cup cooked corn kernels
- 2 large tomatoes, seeded and diced
- I ripe Hass avocado, cut into small pieces
- 1/2 cup finely diced red onion
- 2 cloves garlic, minced
- I jalapeño chile, seeded and finely chopped*
- 1/4 cup lime juice
- 2 tablespoons chopped fresh cilantro
- I teaspoon sea salt

* For added heat, include the seeds

Avocado adds creamy richness to this flavorful salsa, which gets an added spark of heat from the jalapeño. Sweet corn kernels offer a bit of sweetness and welcomed crunch!

1. Place all of the ingredients in a medium bowl and mix well.
2. Cover and refrigerate for at least 1 hour.
3. Serve chilled. Store in the refrigerator up to one day.

CHANGE IT UP . . .

- For added flavor and texture, add a cup of black beans or chopped cucumbers to the mixture.
- Replace the red onion with sliced scallions for milder flavor.

Mango Salsa

Yield: About 2 1/2 cups

- 6 medium tomatoes, seeded and diced
- 2 mangos, diced
- I cup finely diced red onion
- 1/2 cup chopped fresh cilantro
- 1/4 cup red wine vinegar or apple cider vinegar
- 1/2 teaspoon cayenne pepper, or more to taste

This luscious mango-sweetened salsa is best served chilled.

1. Place all of the ingredients in a medium bowl and mix well.
2. Cover and refrigerate for at least 1 hour.
3. Serve chilled. Store in the refrigerator up to five days.

CHANGE IT UP . . .

- To spice up this salsa even further, add a seeded, finely chopped jalapeño chile (or two).

Refreshing Red Grape Salsa

Be sure to try this fresh salsa on crisp Belgian endive leaves.

1. Cut the grapes in half and place in a medium bowl along with the remaining ingredients. Mix well.

2. Cover and refrigerate for at least 1 hour.

3. Serve chilled. Store in the refrigerator up to five days.

Yield: About 2¹/₂ cups

I cup seedless red grapes

4 medium tomatoes, seeded and diced

¹/₂ cup finely diced red onion

2 cloves garlic, minced

2 tablespoons chopped fresh cilantro

2 tablespoons lime juice

I teaspoon sea salt

I teaspoon Tabasco or other hot sauce

Chunky Corn Relish

Fresh cucumber and bits of onion add to the crunchy texture of this flavorful relish. It's great on chips and crackers or plain right from the bowl!

1. Place all of the ingredients in a medium bowl and mix well.

2. Serve as is or refrigerate and serve cold. Store in the refrigerator up to one week.

CHANGE IT UP . . .

• For added flavor, use diced pickles (sweet or dill) instead of cucumbers.

Yield: About 5 cups

4 cups cooked corn kernels

I cup finely chopped yellow onion

I small clove garlic, minced

¹/₂ cup diced cucumber

¹/₄ cup finely chopped fresh parsley

¹/₄ cup lemon juice

¹/₄ cup extra-virgin olive oil

I teaspoon sea salt

Yield: About 1 1/2 cups

2 jalapeño chiles, seeded and coarsely chopped

2 cloves garlic, minced

1/2 cup loosely packed cilantro leaves

2 tablespoons extra-virgin olive oil

15-ounce can black beans, rinsed and drained

1 tablespoon lime juice, or to taste

1 teaspoon sea salt

Jalapeño Bean Dip

*Surround this fiesta favorite with crunchy corn chips—
then watch it disappear before your eyes!
Also makes a great filling for burritos and taquitos.*

1. Place the chiles, garlic, cilantro, and oil in a blender or food processor, and blend about 20 seconds or until fairly smooth.

2. Add the beans, lime juice, and salt to the blender. Pulse a few seconds to form a chunky purée.

3. Serve at room temperature. Store in the refrigerator up to five days.

CHANGE IT UP . . .

- For added tartness, use lemon juice instead of lime juice.

- For a delicious variation, substitute chickpeas for the black beans.

CHILE PEPPERS AND YOUR HEALTH

We are big fans of chile peppers. They're hot and spicy and perfect for livening up lots of different dishes. They come in hundreds of different varieties that vary in shape, color, size, flavor, and heat level. As an added bonus, they're good for you!

The hot and pungent spark found in peppers like jalapeño, ancho, cayenne, and serrano comes from a natural plant compound or phytochemical called *capsaicin*. As a general rule of thumb, the hotter the pepper, the more capsaicin it contains. Researchers have discovered that whether eaten raw, cooked, or added to food as a dried powder, cap-

No-Egg Eggplant Dip

*Great with crackers and rice cakes, this savory dip
is also delicious with fresh cucumber slices,
celery sticks, and crisp Belgian endive leaves.*

1. Preheat the oven to 375°F.

2. Place the eggplant on a baking sheet and place in the oven. Turning occasionally, bake for 50 to 60 minutes or until tender when pierced with a fork. Remove and let cool.

3. Cut the cooled eggplant in half lengthwise. Scoop out the pulp into a large mixing bowl and coarsely mash with a fork. Discard the skin.

4. Add the remaining ingredients and stir well. Cover and refrigerate at least 1 hour.

5. Serve chilled. Store in the refrigerator up to five days.

Yield: About 3 cups

. . . .

1 large eggplant

1 cup diced tomatoes

1/2 cup finely chopped yellow onion

1/4 cup finely chopped parsley

1/4 cup red wine vinegar

2 tablespoons extra-virgin olive oil

1/2 teaspoon garlic powder (optional)

1/4 teaspoon dried oregano

1/4 teaspoon black pepper

1/4 teaspoon sea salt

saicin, which is also available as a supplement, has a number of powerful health benefits.

Studies have shown that, among its impressive effects, capsaicin has been found to help lower cholesterol and blood pressure, which, in turn, improves heart health. It has also been touted for relieving and preventing migraine, cluster, and sinus headaches; for fighting infections; and for reducing the joint pain from arthritis. It also decreases inflammation within the body—a precursor to a heart disease and number of cancers. Capsaicin also speeds up the body's metabolism, which helps burn calories and fat.

Chile peppers—they're small but powerful. We recommend them for spicing up both your meals and your life!

Velvety White Bean Dip

Fennel gives this creamy dip a mild licorice taste.
Perfect with raw veggies, crackers, or rice cakes.

Yield: About 3 cups

$^1/_4$ cup extra-virgin olive oil

2 cloves garlic, minced

1 large fennel bulb, halved lengthwise, cored, and roughly chopped (reserve fronds for garnish)

$^1/_4$ cup water

15-ounce can white beans (Great Northern or cannellini), rinsed and drained

2 tablespoons lemon juice

1 teaspoon sea salt

$^1/_4$ teaspoon black pepper

1. Heat the oil in a medium skillet over medium-low heat. Add the garlic and sauté 1 to 2 minutes, or until it becomes fragrant and begins to brown.

2. Remove the garlic with a slotted spoon and place in a food processor or blender. Set aside.

3. Add the fennel to the same skillet and place over medium heat. Stirring occasionally, cook the fennel about 5 minutes or until it browns lightly around the edges and begins to smell sweet.

4. Add the water to the skillet, bring to a simmer, and cook the fennel about 5 minutes or until the water evaporates and the fennel is soft.

5. Transfer the fennel to the food processor along with the white beans, lemon juice, salt, and pepper. Purée until smooth and velvety.

6. Transfer the dip to a serving bowl and garnish with some of the feathery fennel fronds. Serve immediately or refrigerate and serve chilled. Store in the refrigerator up to five days.

Black Bean and Sun-Dried Tomato Dip

Thick and spicy, this fiber-rich dip packs a flavorful punch. Try spooning some on rice cakes, then top with slices of creamy avocado. Deeelicious!

1. Cut the sun-dried tomatoes into small pieces and set aside.

2. Heat the oil in a skillet over medium-low heat. Add the onion, and sauté about 3 minutes or beginning to soften. Add the garlic and tomatoes, and continue to sauté another 1 or 2 minutes. Remove from the heat and set aside.

3. Place the black beans in medium bowl and mash with a fork (this can be as smooth or as chunky as you like). Add the onion-tomato mixture, chili powder, and salt, and stir well.

4. Transfer to a serving bowl and enjoy warm or at room temperature. Store in the refrigerator up to five days.

CHANGE IT UP . . .

- For super-smooth version, purée the beans in a blender or food processor. Add the remaining ingredients and blend to the desired consistency.

Yield: About 1 1/2 cups

1/2 cup marinated sun-dried tomatoes

1 tablespoon extra-virgin olive oil

1/2 cup finely diced yellow onion

3 cloves garlic, minced

15-ounce can black beans, rinsed and drained

1 teaspoon ground cumin

1/4 teaspoon chili powder

1/4 teaspoon sea salt

A WORD ABOUT SUN-DRIED TOMATOES

When choosing commercial brands of marinated sun-dried tomatoes, be sure to read labels carefully for possible hidden allergens. Also choose those packed in olive oil.

You can also easily reconstitute dried tomatoes at home. Simply place them in a heatproof bowl, cover with boiling water, and let soak 30 minutes or until they are soft and pliable.

Fresh Herb Pesto

*Pine nuts and Parmesan cheese are key ingredients
in traditional pesto. In this allergen-free version,
toasted sunflower seeds replace the nuts—
and it's so flavorful, the cheese will never be missed.*

Yield: About 1 $^1/_2$ cups

$^1/_2$ cup toasted sunflower
seeds

1 clove garlic, minced

1 $^1/_4$ cups loosely packed
fresh basil leaves

3 scallions, coarsely
chopped

$^1/_4$ cup fresh parsley
leaves

2 tablespoons lemon juice

$^1/_4$ teaspoon sea salt

3 tablespoons extra-virgin
olive oil

1. Place all of the ingredients except the oil in a food processor or
   blender. Process until the herbs are finely minced. With the motor
   running, slowly add the olive oil in a thin steady stream. Process
   until smooth and well blended.

2. Transfer the mixture to a bowl and serve with raw vegetables
   and/or crackers, or toss with rice pasta or another gluten-free
   variety. Store in the refrigerator up to five days.

CHANGE IT UP . . .

- For added flavor, blend a few pitted black olives with the other
  ingredients.

- If tree nuts are not an allergy concern, use toasted pine nuts
  instead of sunflower seeds.

- If dairy is not an allergy concern, stir a tablespoon of grated
  Parmesan cheese into the pesto.

Garlicky Roasted Eggplant Dip

The longer this dip sits, the more flavorful it becomes.
That's why we recommend making it the day
before you plan to serve it.

1. Preheat the oven to 375°F.

2. Cut the eggplants in half lengthwise, and lightly brush the cut sides with some of the olive oil. Place the halves cut-side down on a baking sheet.

3. Roast the eggplant for 30 to 40 minutes or until tender when pierced with a fork. Remove and let cool about 15 minutes.

4. While the eggplant is cooling, heat the remaining olive oil in a medium skillet over medium-low heat. Add the onion and garlic, and sauté about 3 minutes or until the onion begins to soften. Add the bell peppers, and continue to sauté another 2 to 3 minutes or until the onion is soft and translucent. Remove and set aside.

5. Scoop the pulp from the eggplant into the bowl of a food processor. Add the sautéed onion mixture, lemon juice, cinnamon (if using), and salt, and process to the desired consistency.

6. Transfer to a bowl, cover, and refrigerate at least 1 hour before serving. (Best if allowed to sit longer to allow the flavors to blend.)

7. Serve chilled or at room temperature. Store in the refrigerator up to five days.

Yield: About 3 cups

2 medium eggplants (about 1 1/2 pounds total weight)

1 cup finely diced yellow onion

2–3 tablespoons extra-virgin olive oil, divided

6 large cloves garlic, minced

1/2 cup roasted red bell peppers

1/2 cup lemon juice

1 teaspoon cinnamon (optional)

1 teaspoon sea salt

2 tablespoons minced fresh parsley for garnish

Mummy's Yummy Hummus

Packed with protein, fiber, vitamins, and minerals, hummus is very versatile. Enjoy it as a dip with raw veggies, chips, and crackers; as a hearty spread for your favorite sandwiches; and as a delicious filling for pitas and tortillas.

Yield: About 3 cups

$^1/_2$ cup tahini (sesame seed butter)

$^1/_4$ cup extra-virgin olive oil

$^1/_4$ cup warm water

$^1/_8$ cup lemon juice

2 cans (15 ounces each) chickpeas, rinsed and drained

2 small cloves garlic, minced

$^1/_2$ teaspoon ground cumin

$^1/_2$ teaspoon sea salt

Pinch black pepper

1. Place the tahini, oil, water, and lemon juice in a blender or food processor, and blend for 30 seconds.

2. Add half the chickpeas and blend another 30 seconds. Add the remaining chickpeas and continue to blend to the desired consistency.

3. Add the garlic, cumin, salt, and pepper, and blend an additional 10 seconds.

4. Transfer the mixture to a covered container and refrigerate at least 3 hours. Serve chilled. Store in the refrigerator up to five days.

CHANGE IT UP . . .

- For nuttier flavor, substitute sesame oil for the olive oil.

- Instead of raw garlic, use 3 roasted cloves for a milder flavor. (For roasting instructions, see page 52.)

- For added flavor and texture, stir 2 tablespoons of finely chopped sun-dried tomatoes into the blended mixture.

Roasted Bell Pepper Hummus

Although you can use any color bell pepper for this recipe,
we prefer the red variety for its mild sweet flavor.

1. Seed and chop the bell pepper, and place in a blender or food processor. Add half the chickpeas and all of the remaining ingredients. Process until very smooth.

2. Add the remaining chickpeas and continue to blend to the desired consistency.

3. Serve immediately or refrigerate and serve chilled. Store in the refrigerator up to five days.

Yield: About 1 1/2 cups

1 medium red bell pepper, roasted (see below)

15-ounce can chickpeas, rinsed and drained

2 tablespoons tahini (sesame seed butter)

1/4 cup extra-virgin olive oil

2 tablespoons lemon juice

2 cloves garlic, minced

1/2 teaspoon sea salt

ROASTING PEPPERS

Roasting gives bell peppers a wonderful mellow smoky flavor and velvety texture. Although jarred varieties are readily available, you can prepare your own in less than thirty minutes. And it's so easy! You can roast them under an oven broiler, on a barbecue grill, or over the open flame of a gas burner.

When using a broiler or grill, cut the peppers in half or quarters, remove the stems and seeds, and place them 4 to 5 inches from the heat source (skin side up under a broiler, and skin side down on a grill). Roast for 5 to 7 minutes, or until the peppers are soft and the skin is blistered and blackened.

When using a gas burner, roast the pepper whole. First, make a small cut near the stem to allow the steam to escape. Using tongs, hold the pepper over a medium flame (or place it right on the burner), frequently turning until the skin is blistered and blackened.

Whether you've used a broiler, grill, or open flame, immediately place the hot cooked peppers in a sealed plastic bag or under an inverted bowl for about 10 minutes. This will trap the steam and loosen the skin. When they are cool enough to handle, peel off the skin.

You can use the peppers immediately or refrigerate them in a sealed container for up to a week. You can also marinate them in a little oil and vinegar or your favorite dressing. Roasted peppers also freeze beautifully.

Garlicky White Bean and Basil Spread

Yield: About 2 cups

- - - - - - - - - - -

2 cans (15 ounces each) cannellini or Great Northern beans, rinsed and drained

6 cloves roasted garlic

3 tablespoons chopped fresh basil

1/4 cup extra-virgin olive oil

3/4 teaspoon sea salt

1/4 teaspoon ground black pepper

Fresh basil and roasted garlic add great flavor to this rich bean spread. Try it as a filling for crisp celery stalks.

1. Place all of the ingredients in a food processor or blender, and process about 30 seconds or until smooth.

2. Serve immediately or refrigerate and serve chilled. Store in the refrigerator up to five days.

CHANGE IT UP . . .

- For a more garlicky spread, use 2 or 3 cloves minced raw garlic instead of roasted.

- Add some finely chopped roasted bell peppers for a flavorful change.

ROASTING GARLIC

Universally popular, roasted garlic is especially appreciated by allergen-free cooks. When slow-roasted, the pungent cloves become mellow melt-in-your-mouth morsels that are deliciously versatile. You can spread them on rice cakes, crackers, and gluten-free bread; add them to soups and savory dishes; and even enjoy them as flavorful pizza toppers.

You can also choose from the two most common garlic types—cloved and elephant—each of which comes in a number of varieties. The papery bulbs of cloved garlic range in color from white and creamy beige to reddish purple, with cloves that range in size as well. Characteristically pungent when raw, the cloves become honeyed and nutty-flavored when roasted. Elephant garlic, on the other hand, is several times larger than common cloved garlic, but much milder and more subtle in flavor with a

Easy Guacamole

Traditionally served with crisp corn chips, this classic guacamole is a snack-time favorite. Try adding a spoonful or two to a fresh green salad or serve some alongside tacos and burritos.

Yield: About 2^1/$_2$ cups

· · · · · · · · · ·

3 ripe Hass avocados

1 large tomato, diced

^{1}/$_4$ cup finely diced onion

3 tablespoons lemon or lime juice

1 clove garlic, minced

1 teaspoon sea salt

1. Cut the avocados in half. Spoon the flesh into a large bowl and mash with a fork (as smooth or chunky as you like). Reserve one of the seeds.

2. Add the remaining ingredients and stir well.

3. Serve immediately or refrigerate and serve chilled. If refrigerating, transfer the guacamole to an airtight container, place the reserved seed in the middle, and cover. (The seed will help prevent it from turning brown.) It will keep about one day.

CHANGE IT UP . . .

- For a spicy kick, add one (or more) of the following: ^{1}/$_4$ cup salsa, 1 teaspoon finely chopped jalapeño chile, or ^{1}/$_4$ teaspoon cayenne pepper.

taste that is similar to leeks. Roasting results in an even milder taste for these colossal cloves. Both garlic varieties are delicious, depending on your preference.

Although special garlic roasters are available, they aren't necessary. Just follow these simple steps:

1. Remove the loose papery outer skin from a head of garlic, but don't peel or separate the cloves. Cut off about ^{1}/$_4$ inch from the top to expose some of the cloves.

2. Place the entire head on a piece of aluminum foil, and drizzle with a little olive oil (a teaspoon or so). Seal the head in the foil, and roast in a 375°F oven for 40 to 45 minutes or until the cloves are soft.

3. Remove the roasted cloves from their skins either with a knife, or by squeezing them out with your fingertips.

4. Store in a covered container and refrigerate for a few days, or freeze up to six months.

Tasty Taquitos

*Traditional Mexican taquitos are small rolled-up corn tortillas
with meat and/or cheese filling. They are usually fried and
served hot and crisp. In this lower-fat baked version,
the filling is made with pinto beans and vegan cheddar.
Everyone can enjoy these savory snacks.*

Yield: 12 taquitos

16-ounce can refried
pinto beans

$3/4$ cup soy-free vegan
cheddar cheese shreds

3 tablespoons finely
chopped mild chiles
(optional)

1 tablespoon lime juice

12 corn tortillas
(6-inch rounds)

Olive oil cooking spray

1. Preheat the oven to 400°F. Lightly oil a baking sheet or cover with a sheet of parchment paper. Set aside.

2. To prepare the filling, place the beans, cheese, chiles (if using), and lime juice in a medium bowl and mix well. Set aside.

3. Warm the tortillas one at a time in a dry skillet over medium heat until soft and pliable—about 15 to 20 seconds on each side.

4. Spread 1 heaping tablespoon of filling in an even layer over half of the warm tortilla. Beginning at the filled half, roll it up tightly to form a cigar-shaped cylinder.

5. Place the filled tortilla seam side down on the prepared baking sheet. Repeat with the remaining tortillas and filling, then spray them generously with cooking spray.

6. Bake for 20 to 25 minutes or until browned and crisp. Let cool about 5 minutes before serving with your favorite salsa and/or guacamole. We recommend the Super Salsa (page 42) and Easy Guacamole (page 53).

CHANGE IT UP . . .

- For a more bite-sized snack, cut the taquitos in half before serving.

- For spicier version, add a small finely chopped jalapeño chile or $1/4$ teaspoon cayenne pepper to the filling.

- Include $1/2$ teaspoon ground cumin for added flavor.

Simple Oven-Crisp Potato Skins

Whether served hot from the oven or at room temperature, these simple potato skins are always a hit.

1. Preheat the oven to 450°F.

2. Pierce the potatoes in several places with the tines of a fork or the tip of a small knife, then lightly coat the skins with cooking spray.

3. Place the potatoes on the center rack of the oven, and bake for 40 to 45 minutes or until fork tender.

4. When the potatoes are cool enough to handle, quarter them lengthwise into wedges. With a spoon, carefully remove most of the flesh, leaving about $1/4$-inch on the skins.

5. Lightly coat the wedges with cooking spray, and sprinkle with garlic powder and salt. Arrange on a baking sheet and return to the oven.

6. Bake the skins for 7 to 10 minutes or until hot and crisp.

7. Arrange on a platter, garnish with scallions, and serve.

Yield: 16 potato skins

• • • • • • • • • •

4 medium baking potatoes

Olive oil cooking spray

1 teaspoon garlic powder

Sea salt to taste

Finely chopped scallions for garnish

CHANGE IT UP . . .

• Sprinkle the wedges with shredded soy-free vegan cheddar or mozzarella before baking.

• Serve plain or top with a spoonful of your favorite salsa or dip. The choices in this chapter are all good options.

Baked Tortilla Chips

Nothing can be easier to make than these crunchy tortilla chips. They go with just about any dip, salsa, or spread, and lend themselves to lots of flavorful variations.

Yield: 80 chips

10 corn tortillas
(6-inch rounds)

3 tablespoons extra-virgin
olive oil

1 teaspoon sea salt

1. Preheat the oven to 350°F. Line a baking sheet with parchment paper and set aside.

2. Coat both sides of the tortillas with oil, and then cut each into 8 triangles. Place on the baking sheet and sprinkle with salt.

3. Bake for 10 to 12 minutes or until crisp. Serve warm or at room temperature.

CHANGE IT UP . . .

- For a spicy spark, add a few sprinkles of chili powder before baking. For a garlicky version, sprinkle with garlic powder.

- For lime-flavored chips, mix 2 tablespoons lime juice with the oil. Or, for an acidic burst of flavor, add 1 tablespoon balsamic vinegar to the oil.

Krispy Kale Chips

These mineral-rich crisps are a crunchy alternative to potato chips. And they are SO simple to make!

Yield: 6 servings

12 ounces kale (1 large
bunch) stemmed and
chopped into 1-inch pieces

1/4 cup extra-virgin
olive oil

1 teaspoon sea salt
or to taste

1. Preheat the oven to 350°F. Line a baking sheet with parchment paper and set aside.

2. Place the kale in a large bowl. Drizzle with the oil and toss well. Sprinkle with salt and toss again.

3. Spread out the kale on the prepared baking sheet in a single layer (you may have to do this in two batches).

4. Place on a rack in the middle of the oven and bake 8 to 10 minutes. Toss the chips with a spatula and bake another 4 to 6 minutes or until crisp. (Be careful not to burn.)

5. Serve warm or at room temperature.

CHANGE IT UP . . .

* For a different flavor, toss the kale with a blend of 3 tablespoons olive oil, 2 tablespoons apple cider vinegar, and 2 tablespoons honey.

* Along with the salt, sprinkle the kale with a teaspoon of garlic powder. Or add a little chili powder to the salt for spicy chips.

Crunchy Croutons

These gluten-free croutons are great additions to soups, salads, and stews. They're also terrific little "snackers" to enjoy on their own.

1. Preheat the oven to 300°F. Line a baking sheet with parchment paper and set aside.

2. Place the oil, salt, seasoning blend, and onion powder in a medium mixing bowl and whisk until well blended. Add the bread cubes and toss to coat.

3. Arrange the bread cubes in a single layer on the prepared baking sheet.

4. Bake for 35 to 40 minutes or until the cubes are dry and golden brown. Toss occasionally with a spatula as they bake.

5. Remove from the oven and cool completely. Store in an airtight container in the pantry up to two weeks.

Yield: About 4 cups

4 cups cubed rice bread ($1/2$-inch cubes)

$1/2$ cup extra-virgin olive oil

1 teaspoon sea salt

1 teaspoon dried Italian seasoning blend

1 teaspoon onion powder

CHANGE IT UP . . .

* Use your favorite dry herbs and seasonings for these croutons. Chile powder, garlic powder, and dried rosemary are just a few suggestions.

Aztec Corn Cakes

*Made with amaranth, an ancient grain of Mexico, these
gluten-free corn cakes are perfect to serve with your favorite
spread or salsa. Try them with our Super Salsa (page 42) or
topped with a generous spread of Jalapeño Bean Dip (page 44).
They are also great with hearty stews and dishes like
the Pinto Bean and Sweet Potato Chili (page 128).*

Yield: 5 to 6 cakes

I cup yellow cornmeal

³/₄ cup amaranth flour

I ¹/₂ cups Nanz' Vegetable
Stock (page 64), or
commercial variety

I tablespoon extra-virgin
olive oil

I small yellow onion,
diced

¹/₄ cup finely diced
Anaheim chiles

I garlic clove, minced

¹/₂ teaspoon chili powder

¹/₄ teaspoon sea salt

¹/₄ teaspoon ground cumin

¹/₄ teaspoon black pepper

1. Combine the cornmeal and amaranth flour in a large bowl and
   set aside.

2. Bring the stock to a boil, add it to the cornmeal mixture, and stir
   well. (The consistency will be thick.) Set aside.

3. Heat the oil in medium pot over medium heat. Add the onion,
   chiles, and garlic, and sauté 3 to 5 minutes or until soft. Add the
   chili powder, salt, cumin, and pepper, and stir well.

4. Fold the sautéed onion-chile mixture into the cornmeal mixture
   to form a thick batter.

5. Form the batter into 3-inch-round patties about ¹/₂ inch thick. Add
   them to a heated, lightly oiled skillet over medium-high heat, and
   cook 2 to 3 minutes on each side or until lightly browned.

6. Serve warm or at room temperature.

Light 'n Flaky Oat Crisps

These crispy crackers are perfect with dips or to enjoy alone.

Yield: About 32 crackers

1 1/2 cups rolled oats

1 cup brown rice flour

1/4 teaspoon sea salt

1/4 cup extra-virgin olive oil

1/2 cup water

1. Preheat the oven to 350°F. Lightly oil a baking sheet or line with parchment paper. Set aside.

2. Place the oats in a blender or food processor and grind to a coarse powder.

3. Transfer the oats to a large bowl, add the brown rice flour and sea salt, and stir until well combined.

4. While continuing to stir the flour, slowly add the olive oil until the mixture resembles coarse crumbs. Add the water and stir to form a ball of dough.

5. Knead the dough lightly, then roll or press it into a square or rectangle about 1/8 inch thick. With a sharp knife or pizza cutter, cut the flattened dough into 2-inch squares.

6. Place the squares on the prepared baking sheet, and prick the tops with a fork to prevent them from blistering and bubbling up as they bake.

7. Bake the crackers for 12 to 15 minutes, or until the edges are slightly brown. Cool before serving.

IMPORTANT WORD ABOUT OATS

When purchasing oats or oat flour, it is important to be aware that they are sometimes processed in facilities that also handle wheat (and/or other gluten-containing grains like rye and barley), so cross-contamination may occur. Be sure to purchase varieties that are labeled wheat-free or gluten-free.

Mini Crunch Cups

Noted vegan chef Vicki Chelf created the recipe for these tiny snack cups, which are prebaked and can hold all sorts of delicious fillings—both savory and sweet. Hummus and other thick spreads, creamy mashed avocado, and even applesauce or puréed fruit make great fillings. This recipe is also easily doubled.

Yield: 12 mini cups

3/4 cup rolled oats

1/4 cup flaxseed meal

1/4 teaspoon sea salt

1 tablespoon extra-virgin olive oil

3–4 tablespoons water

1. Preheat the oven to 350°F. Lightly oil 12 cups of a mini muffin tin and set aside.

2. Add the oats to a blender or food processor and grind for 25 to 30 seconds to a coarse flour.

3. Add the flaxseed meal and salt to the blender, and process with the oat flour for 15 to 20 seconds. Transfer to a medium mixing bowl.

4. Cut the olive oil into the flax-oat mixture with a fork until well distributed.

5. Stir the water into the mixture 1 tablespoon at a time until it becomes firm enough to hold a shape when pressed together with your hands. (Don't expect it to resemble smooth kneadable dough. It will be somewhat coarse and crumbly.)

6. Press the mixture into a 12-inch-long roll. Cut the roll into 12 pieces (1-inch long) and place one piece in each of the oiled muffin cups. Press the mixture on the bottom and sides of each cup in an even thickness (about 1/8 inch).

7. Bake the cups for 18 to 20 minutes or until browned and crisp. Let cool about 5 minutes before removing from the tin. If necessary, run a knife around the edges to loosen.

8. Allow the cups to cool completely before filling. Store unfilled leftovers in an airtight container up to three days.

CHANGE IT UP . . .

- For a different flavor, add a tablespoon of sesame seeds, poppy seeds, or caraway seeds in Step 3.

- If using the cups for puréed fruit or other sweet filling, omit the salt and add $1/2$ teaspoon ground cinnamon in Step 3.

- For larger cups, double the recipe and bake in a standard muffin tin. This will yield 9 cups.

- When doubled, this recipe makes enough for a standard 9-inch pie crust, which you can either prebake or fill and bake like a conventional pie. Makes a great crust for quiche (if eggs are not an allergen).

Brown Rice Chia Crisps

With a taste similar to pita chips, these crunchy crisps go great with the salsas, dips, and spreads in this chapter, as well as your favorite soups and salads.

1. Preheat the oven to 350°F. Line a baking sheet with parchment paper and set aside.

2. Coat both sides of the tortillas with oil, then cut each into 16 thin wedges. (We use a pizza cutter for this.)

3. Place the wedges on the prepared baking sheet. Mix together the chia seeds, salt, and curry powder, then sprinkle over the wedges.

4. Bake for 8 to 10 minutes or until crisp.

5. Serve warm or at room temperature.

Yield: 32 crisps

2 brown rice tortillas (6-inch rounds)

2 tablespoons extra-virgin olive oil

1 teaspoon chia seeds

$1/2$ teaspoon sea salt, or to taste

$1/8$ teaspoon curry powder

CHANGE IT UP . . .

- For a salt-free version, replace the salt with dry herb seasoning.

- This recipe also works well with corn tortillas and flaxseeds.

5

Super Soups

Is there anything more hypnotic than the heady aroma of homemade soup as it gently simmers on the stove? Mmm, soup. The very word conjures images of warmth and comfort. Whether thick and hearty or light and brothy, homemade soup—always a welcome choice—seems to magically nourish the body as well as the soul. It's also easy to make, economical, and lends itself to creativity. You can add a little of this or toss in a bit of that to come up with new twists on the same recipe. Best of all, it gives you control over the ingredients—a critical factor when cooking allergen-free.

Because we believe the best soups start with a rich, flavorful stock, this chapter starts off with a basic family recipe that we've used for years. Along with serving as a great foundation for soups and stews, a good stock also adds welcomed richness to rice dishes, vegetables, and many other savory choices.

What follows next is a wide selection of our favorite soup sensations, something to satisfy every mood. If it's a light, brothy soup you want, there are choices like the sweet, delicate Savoy Cabbage Soup and the vegetable-rich Springtime Soup. Among the heartier soups, there's Cannellini and Pasta, as well as the classic Mighty Minestrone. If you're craving something rich and creamy, be sure to give the Butternut Squash or the Cauliflower Curry Soup a try.

For those hot summer days when a cold soup is the perfect choice, we've shared two versions of refreshing gazpacho. There's also a recipe for luscious split pea soup that get a smoky spark of heat from chipotle chiles, a creamy tomato soup that's a lunchtime favorite, and many, many more. There's even a Mexican-inspired soup complete with tortilla chips. *Olé!*

No matter what type of soup suits your mood, you're sure to find it in this chapter. So let's get started. Time to pull out the soup pot and get simmering.

Nanz' Vegetable Stock

Yield: 8 cups (2 quarts)

8 cups cold water

5 carrots, halved

4 tomatoes, halved or quartered

4 stalks celery (with leafy tops), halved

3 medium onions, halved

4 cloves garlic, minced (optional)

3 sprigs fresh parsley

2 teaspoons sea salt, or to taste

This flavorful stock is named after our beloved grandmother,
Giovanna Ziara Muzio (better known as "Nanz"),
who used it as the basis for many of her homemade soups.
Feel free to double this basic recipe, then freeze portions
for later use. For additional preparation pointers,
see "About Homemade Stock" below.

1. Place all of the ingredients in a large pot and bring to a boil over high heat. Reduce the heat to low, cover, and simmer for about 1 hour.

2. Pour the contents of the pot into a sieve or colander that has been set over a pot or heatproof bowl. Discard the vegetables.

3. The stock is now ready to use. To store for later use, first allow it to cool to room temperature, then store in sealed containers. Refrigerate up to one week or freeze up to a year.

ABOUT HOMEMADE STOCK

A great foundation for soups and stews, a flavorful stock also adds welcomed richness to rice dishes, vegetables, and many other savory choices. Although commercially prepared stocks are readily available, making your own puts you in control of the ingredients—and guarantees that it's allergen-free. It's also a great way to use up those leftover vegetables.

In this chapter, we've shared our basic recipe—Nanz' Vegetable Stock (above). But keep in mind that when it comes to preparing stock, there is no single recipe. What goes in it will depend on what you have on hand—including "scraps" like carrot peels and heels, celery tops, and even onion skins! Use our basic recipe as a starting point for experimenting with your own ingredient choices.

When using root vegetables like carrots, turnips, and parsnips, peeling isn't necessary, just be sure to scrub them well. To further elevate the flavor of a basic

Creamed Corn Chowder

*This luscious chowder is satisfyingly
rich and creamy.*

1. Place the beans in a mixing bowl and mash well with a fork until creamy. Set aside.

2. Heat the oil in a large pot over medium-low heat. Add the onion and celery, and sauté for 3 to 5 minutes or until soft.

3. Add the mashed beans and all of the remaining ingredients to the pot. Increase the heat to high, cover, and bring to a boil. Reduce the heat to low, and simmer for 20 to 25 minutes or until the vegetables are tender.

4. Serve piping hot.

Yield: 4 to 6 servings

15-ounce can cannellini or Great Northern beans, rinsed and drained

2 tablespoons extra-virgin olive oil

1 large yellow onion, finely chopped

2 stalks celery, coarsely chopped

1 large russet potato, peeled and cut into small cubes

4 cups corn kernels

4 cups Nanz' Vegetable Stock (page 64), or commercial variety

1 teaspoon sea salt

vegetable stock, try adding dried mushrooms and various herbs and/or spices. And for added depth and richness, roast or sauté the vegetables before cooking them in the stock.

Whenever you prepare fresh vegetables, we recommend saving the peels and other scraps in a plastic ziplock bag in the freezer, and then continue adding to it. And don't throw out those carrots and celery stalks that are getting soft, or that onion that is past its prime—clean them up and add them to the bag as well. The next time you make stock, you can add these bits and pieces to the pot.

Not only is homemade stock simple to prepare (and guaranteed allergen-free), it is also healthier and more flavorful than most commercial varieties. As an added bonus, it is less expensive. After making the stock, we recommend portioning it into various sized containers to store in the freezer. That way, you'll always have some on hand to use at a moment's notice. Be sure to give it a try.

Creamy Tomato Soup

*Rich and creamy, this classic tomato soup
has long been a lunchtime staple in our homes.
A true family favorite!*

Yield: 3 to 4 servings

1 tablespoon extra-virgin olive oil

1 medium onion, diced

2 cloves garlic, minced

28-ounce can whole tomatoes, not drained

1 cup Nanz' Vegetable Stock (page 64), or commercial variety

1/4 cup chopped fresh basil

1 teaspoon fresh thyme

1 teaspoon sea salt

1 cup rice milk

1/8 teaspoon black pepper

1. Heat the oil in a medium pot over medium-low heat. Add the onion and garlic, and sauté 2 to 3 minutes or until beginning to soften.

2. Add the tomatoes, stock, basil, thyme, and salt. Increase the heat to high, and bring to a boil over high heat. Reduce the heat to low, cover, and simmer for 15 to 20 minutes. Add the rice milk and pepper, and stir well.

3. Transfer the soup to a blender or food processor and blend until smooth and creamy.

4. Return the blended soup to the pot, and heat before serving.

CHANGE IT UP . . .

- Try this soup chilled. It's especially refreshing on hot days.

- For a bit of crunch and visual appeal, break up a rice cake and scatter the pieces over individual servings.

Creamy Roasted Garlic Soup

The nutty flavor of roasted garlic is spotlighted in this delicious soup, which gets it creamy richness from puréed cauliflower and potatoes.

Yield: 6 to 8 servings

2 tablespoons extra-virgin olive oil

1 medium onion, diced

2 stalks celery, sliced

3 tablespoons fresh thyme or 1 tablespoon dried

6 cups Nanz' Vegetable Stock (page 64), or commercial variety

2 medium russet potatoes, peeled and diced

1 small cauliflower, cut into florets

1 1/2 teaspoons sea salt, or to taste

1 teaspoon Dijon-style mustard

1 teaspoon black pepper

4 heads roasted garlic (see page 52 for roasting instructions)

1. Heat the oil in a large pot over medium-low heat. Add the onion, celery, and thyme, and sauté 2 to 3 minutes or until beginning to soften.

2. Add all of the remaining ingredients to the pot except the garlic. Increase the heat to high, and bring to a boil over high heat. Reduce the heat to low, cover, and simmer 20 to 25 minutes or until the vegetables are tender.

3. Transfer the soup to a blender or food processor and purée until smooth. (You may have to do this in multiple batches.) Add the roasted garlic cloves and continue to blend until smooth.

4. Return the puréed soup to the pot, and heat before serving.

Mighty Minestrone

This traditional Italian vegetable soup is so hearty, it can serve as a meal by itself. It also lasts up to one week in the refrigerator— and the longer it sits, the more flavorful it becomes.

Yield: 6 to 8 servings

2 tablespoons extra-virgin olive oil

I large onion, chopped

I small leek, cleaned well and sliced

2 cloves garlic, minced

2 small zucchini, quartered and sliced

2 medium carrots, sliced

4 $1/4$ cups water or vegetable stock, divided

15-ounce can navy beans or other white beans, rinsed and drained

28-ounce can whole tomatoes, coarsely chopped, not drained

2 cans (15 ounces each) red kidney beans, rinsed and drained

I large russet potato, cut into small cubes

I cup shredded green cabbage

$1/2$ cup green beans (1-inch pieces)

2 tablespoons chopped fresh basil

2 cups spiral- or elbow-shaped rice, corn, or quinoa pasta

2 tablespoons chopped fresh parsley

1. Heat the oil in a large pot over medium-low heat. Add the onion, leek, and garlic, and sauté 2 to 3 minutes or until beginning to soften. Add the zucchini and carrots, and continue to sauté another 2 minutes.

2. While the vegetables are sautéing, purée the navy beans with $1/4$ cup of the water in a blender or food processor, or mash them well with a fork. Add the purée to the pot along with the tomatoes, kidney beans, potato, cabbage, green beans, basil, and the remaining 4 cups of water.

3. Increase the heat to high and bring the ingredients to a boil. Reduce the heat to low, and simmer covered for 45 to 60 minutes or until the vegetables are very tender.

4. While the soup is simmering, cook the pasta according to package directions. Drain and set aside.

5. Add the parsley and pasta to the soup near the end of cooking time. Ladle the piping hot soup into bowls and serve.

Cheesy Broccoli-Potato Soup

Vegan cheddar adds the perfect cheesy touch to this delicious soup.

Yield: 5 to 6 servings

1 1/2 cups fresh broccoli florets

1 tablespoon lemon juice

1 tablespoon extra-virgin olive oil

1 medium onion, diced

2 cloves garlic, minced

3 cups Nanz' Vegetable Stock (page 64), or commercial variety

2 cups diced russet potatoes

1/4 teaspoon ground nutmeg

1/4 teaspoon garlic powder

1 cup rice milk

1 cup soy-free vegan cheddar cheese shreds

1. Bring a medium pot of water to boil. Add the broccoli florets and lemon juice, and cook about 3 minutes, or until slightly cooked and firm yet tender. Drain the broccoli and set aside.

2. Heat the oil in a large pot over medium-low heat. Add the onion and garlic, and sauté 3 to 5 minutes or until soft and translucent.

3. Add the broccoli, stock, potatoes, nutmeg, and garlic powder to the pot. Increase the heat to high, cover, and bring to a boil. Reduce the heat to low and simmer for 15 to 20 minutes or until the potatoes are tender.

4. Stir the rice milk and cheese into the pot, and simmer another 5 minutes. Serve hot.

Roasted Beet Soup

Roasting vegetables brings out their natural sweetness.
This soup highlights a nice variety of roasted veggies with
a special focus on beets. Just be careful—beet juice can
stain your hands as well as clothing, dishtowels, etc.
We usually wear gloves when working with them.

Yield: 5 to 6 servings

3 pounds fresh beets, peeled and cut into bite-sized pieces

1 large onion, diced

2 carrots, cut into $1/4$-inch slices

1 red bell pepper, seeded and chopped

2 tablespoons extra-virgin olive oil

2 cups Nanz' Vegetable Stock (page 64), or commercial variety

2 cups apple juice

1 teaspoon dried tarragon

1 teaspoon sea salt

$1/4$ teaspoon black pepper

1. Preheat the oven to 400°F.

2. Place the beets, onion, carrots, and bell pepper in large bowl. Add the olive oil and toss until well coated.

3. Transfer the vegetables to a large roasting pan, and roast for 35 to 40 minutes or until tender.

4. Place the roasted vegetables in a large pot along with the stock and apple juice, and bring to a boil over high heat. Reduce the heat to low and simmer 20 to 25 minutes. Add the tarragon, salt, and pepper, and continue to simmer another few minutes.

5. Ladle the piping hot soup into bowls and serve.

CHANGE IT UP . . .

- For a smoother version, transfer the cooked soup to a blender or food processor and purée until smooth. (You may have to do this in multiple batches.) Return the soup to the pot and heat before serving.

Savoy Cabbage Soup

Crinkle-leafed Savoy cabbage is milder and more tender than regular white cabbage. It gives this soup a delicate sweet flavor.

Yield: 5 to 6 servings

3 tablespoons extra-virgin olive oil

1 medium head Savoy cabbage, cored and thinly sliced

2 stalks celery, sliced

3 cloves garlic, halved

5 cups Nanz' Vegetable Stock (page 64), or commercial variety

1/2 cup medium- or long-grain rice

1 teaspoon sea salt

Soy-free vegan mozzarella shreds for garnish (optional)

1. Heat the oil in large pot over medium heat. Add the cabbage, celery, and garlic, and sauté 5 to 7 minutes or until beginning to soften.

2. Add the stock, rice, and salt to the pot, and bring to a boil over high heat. Reduce the heat to medium-low, and simmer for 20 to 25 minutes or until the rice is tender.

3. Serve as is or topped with a sprinkling of vegan mozzarella.

White Bean Soup with Swiss chard

*Healthy, hearty, and simple to prepare,
this nourishing soup is warm and comforting.*

Yield: 6 to 8 servings

2 tablespoons extra-virgin olive oil

1 medium onion, diced

4 cloves garlic, minced

$1/2$ teaspoon red pepper flakes

2 medium carrots, sliced

2 stalks celery, sliced

1 teaspoon chopped fresh rosemary

2 cups Nanz' Vegetable Stock (page 64), or commercial variety

2 cans (15 ounces each) diced tomatoes, not drained

$1/2$ cup chopped sun-dried tomatoes

15-ounce can cannellini beans or other white bean, rinsed and drained

Small bunch Swiss chard (about 6 ounces), coarsely chopped

$1/2$ cup chopped fresh basil

1 teaspoon chopped fresh thyme

1. Heat the oil in large pot over medium heat. Add the onion, garlic, and pepper flakes, and sauté 2 to 3 minutes or until the onion begins to soften. Add the carrots, celery, and rosemary, and continue to sauté about 10 minutes or until soft.

2. Add the stock, diced tomatoes, sun-dried tomatoes, and beans to the pot. Stir well.

3. Transfer the soup to a blender or food processor and purée until smooth. (You may have to do this in multiple batches.)

4. Return the puréed mixture to the pot. Add the Swiss chard, basil, and thyme. Simmer over medium heat for 15 to 20 minutes or until the chard is tender.

5. Spoon into bowls and serve.

CHANGE IT UP . . .

- For a chunky brothier version, skip the puréeing. Add the chard, basil, and thyme in Step 2, and cook 15 to 20 minutes or until the chard is tender.

Cauliflower-Curry Soup

Rich, creamy, and full of flavor!

Yield: 6 to 8 servings

2 tablespoons extra-virgin olive oil

1 medium onion, diced

2 cloves garlic, minced

1 large Granny Smith or Pippen apple, peeled and coarsely chopped

1 tablespoon curry powder

1 large head cauliflower, chopped into 1-inch pieces (about 6 cups)

4 cups Nanz' Vegetable Stock (page 64), or commercial variety

1 tablespoon apple cider vinegar

2 tablespoons maple syrup (optional)

1. Heat the oil in large pot over medium-low heat. Add the onion and garlic, and sauté 3 to 5 minutes or until soft. Add the apple and curry powder, stir well, and continue to sauté for 2 to 3 minutes.

2. Add the cauliflower and stock, and bring to a boil over high heat. Reduce the heat to low, cover, and simmer 20 to 25 minutes or until the cauliflower is soft.

3. Transfer the soup to a blender or food processor and purée until smooth. (You may have to do this in multiple batches.)

4. Return the puréed soup to the pot, stir in the vinegar and maple syrup (if using), and heat before serving.

Creamy Carrot-Fennel Soup

Rolled oats add to the creamy goodness of this blended soup.

Yield: 6 to 8 servings

2 tablespoons extra-virgin olive oil

1 medium onion, coarsely chopped

2 cloves garlic, chopped

6 large carrots, chopped

1 medium fennel bulb, finely chopped

6 cups Nanz' Vegetable Stock (page 64), or commercial variety

1/2 cup quick-cooking rolled oats

1 teaspoon sea salt

1. Heat the oil in a large pot over medium-low heat. Add the onion and garlic, and sauté 3 to 5 minutes or until beginning to soften. Add the carrots and fennel, and continue to sauté 15 to 20 minutes or until tender.

2. Add the stock and oats to the pot, and bring to a boil over high heat. Reduce the heat to low, cover, and simmer 15 to 20 minutes or until the vegetables are very soft and tender.

3. Transfer the soup to a blender or food processor and purée until smooth. (You may have to do this in multiple batches.)

4. Return the puréed soup to the pot, stir in the salt, and heat before serving. You can also refrigerate the soup and enjoy it chilled.

Springtime Vegetable Soup

This soup is rich with carrots, green beans, asparagus, and other fresh spring vegetables.

Yield: 6 to 8 servings

2 tablespoons extra-virgin olive oil

4 medium leeks, cleaned well and sliced

6 cups Nanz' Vegetable Stock (page 64), or commercial variety

1 cup diced carrots

1 cup green beans (1-inch pieces)

1 cup diced zucchini

1 cup fresh or frozen green peas

1 cup sliced asparagus

15-ounce can cannellini beans or other white bean, rinsed and drained

2 tablespoons chopped fresh basil

1 tablespoon chopped fresh parsley

3 cloves garlic, minced

1. Heat the oil in a large pot over medium-low heat. Add the leeks, and sauté 3 to 5 minutes or until beginning to soften.

2. Add the stock, carrots, green beans, zucchini, peas, and asparagus to the pot, and bring to a boil over high heat. Reduce the heat to low and simmer for 10 to 15 minutes or until the vegetables are tender.

3. Add the cannellini beans, basil, parsley, and garlic to the pot, and simmer another 5 to 10 minutes.

4. Spoon into bowls and serve.

Smoky Split Pea Soup

*This version of split pea soup gets a smoky spark
of heat from chipotle chiles.*

Yield: 5 to 6 servings

2 tablespoons extra-virgin
olive oil

1 large yellow onion, diced

2 cloves garlic, minced

1 large stalk celery, diced

1 tablespoon chopped
chipotle chiles

1 teaspoon paprika

6 cups Nanz' Vegetable Stock
(page 64), commercial
stock, or water

16-ounce package green
split peas (2¼ cups)

1 teaspoon sea salt,
or to taste

1. Heat the oil in a large pot over medium-low heat. Add the onion, garlic, and celery, and sauté 2 to 3 minutes or until beginning to soften. Add the chipotle chiles and paprika, stir well, and continue to sauté another 3 to 5 minutes.

2. Add the stock, split peas, and salt to the pot, and bring to a boil over high heat. Reduce the heat to low, cover, and simmer about 1 hour or until the soup reaches the desired thickness.

3. Ladle the piping hot soup into bowls and serve.

CHANGE IT UP . . .

- For a milder, more traditional-tasting soup, omit the chipotle chiles and paprika.

- Add a large diced potato to the pot in Step 2. For added sweetness, try a sweet potato.

- Near the end of cooking time, add a 14-ounce can of diced tomatoes to the pot.

Tasty
Tarragon Pea Soup

Tarragon adds a mild anise flavor to this soup,
which is just as delicious chilled as it is piping hot.

Yield: 3 to 4 servings

1 tablespoon extra-virgin olive oil	2 stalks celery, sliced	1 tablespoon chopped fresh tarragon or 1 teaspoon dried
2 medium leeks, cleaned well and thinly sliced	2$^1/_2$ cups Nanz' Vegetable Stock (page 64), or commercial variety	$^1/_2$ teaspoon sea salt
2 cloves garlic, minced	3 cups fresh or frozen peas	$^1/_4$ teaspoon black pepper

1. Heat the oil in large pot over medium-low heat. Add the leeks and garlic, and sauté 5 to 8 minutes or until soft. Add the celery, and continue to sauté another 1 to 2 minutes.

2. Add the stock and peas to the pot, and bring to a boil over high heat. Reduce the heat to low, and simmer 2 to 3 minutes.

3. Stir the tarragon, salt, and pepper into the pot. Transfer the soup to a blender or food processor, and purée until smooth. (You may have to do this in two batches.)

4. Return the puréed soup to the pot, and heat before serving. Also delicious warm (straight from the blender), or chilled.

Favorite Spanish-Style Gazpacho

*Cold and refreshing, this version of the classic Spanish tomato soup
really hits the spot, especially on hot days.*

Yield: 5 to 6 servings

8 large plum tomatoes,
coarsely chopped

5 large scallions, sliced

1 medium cucumber, peeled,
seeded, and chopped

1 small bell pepper, seeded
and coarsely chopped

2 cloves garlic, minced

2 cups tomato juice

$1/4$ cup extra-virgin olive oil

$1/4$ cup lemon juice

2 tablespoons red wine
vinegar

$1 1/2$ teaspoons sea salt

$1/4$ teaspoon cayenne
pepper, or more to taste

Avocado wedges for
garnish

Fresh cilantro for garnish

1. Place all of the ingredients except the avocado and cilantro in a
   blender or food processor, and blend or pulse to the desired
   chunkiness.

2. Transfer the mixture to a large glass bowl (or other type of non-
   reactive material). Refrigerate at least 2 hours or until well chilled.
   (It's best to refrigerate 8 hours or overnight to allow the flavors
   to blend.)

3. Serve cold, topped with a slice of avocado and sprinkling of
   cilantro.

Gazpacho with Avocado and Grapes

*Green grapes replace the traditionally used tomatoes
in this refreshing gazpacho.*

Yield: 4 to 5 servings

1 large cucumber, peeled, seeded, and coarsely chopped

2 cups Nanz' Vegetable Stock (page 64), or commercial variety

2 cups diced green grapes, divided

6 medium scallions, sliced

3 stalks celery, sliced

2 ripe Hass avocados, diced

1 jalapeño pepper, seeded and finely chopped

3 tablespoons lime juice

1/4 cup chopped fresh cilantro

1. Place the cucumber and stock in a blender or food processor, and pulse to a slushy consistency. Add 1 1/2 cups of the grapes and all of the remaining ingredients, and blend or pulse to the desired chunkiness.

2. Transfer the mixture to a large glass bowl (or other type of non-reactive material), and stir in the remaining grapes. Refrigerate at least 2 hours or until well chilled. (It's best to refrigerate 8 hours or overnight to allow the flavors to blend.)

3. Serve cold.

Butternut Squash Soup

Pear is the secret ingredient that enhances the mild sweetness of this creamy puréed soup.

Yield: 6 to 8 servings

3 tablespoons extra-virgin olive oil

2 medium leeks, cleaned well and finely chopped

1 small butternut squash (about 2 pounds), peeled and cut into 1-inch pieces

3 large ripe Bosc pears or other sweet variety, peeled and cut into 1-inch cubes

5 cups Nanz' Vegetable Stock (page 64), or commercial variety

2 cups rice milk or coconut milk

1 teaspoon dried thyme

1 teaspoon dried oregano

1. Heat the oil in a large pot over medium-low heat. Add the leeks and sauté 5 to 8 minutes or until soft. Add the squash and pears, and continue to sauté another 3 to 4 minutes.

2. Add the stock to the pot and bring to a boil over high heat. Reduce the heat to low, cover, and simmer 20 to 25 minutes or until the squash is tender.

3. Stir the rice milk into the pot. Transfer the soup to a blender or food processor, and purée until smooth. (You may have to do this in multiple batches.)

4. Return the puréed soup to the pot, stir in the thyme and oregano, and heat before serving.

Sweet 'n Spicy Carrot Bisque

Rich, creamy, and full of flavor!

Yield: 5 to 6 servings

1 tablespoon extra-virgin olive oil

1 medium yellow onion, diced

2 cloves garlic, minced

2 tablespoons minced fresh ginger

1 tablespoon curry powder

$1/8$ teaspoon cayenne pepper

$4^1/4$ cups water, divided

4 large carrots, sliced into $1/4$-inch rounds

1 medium sweet potato, peeled and cut into small pieces

1 teaspoon sea salt

13.5-ounce can coconut milk

2 tablespoons lime juice

1. Heat the oil in large pot over medium-low heat. Add the onion and garlic, and sauté 2 to 3 minutes or until beginning to soften. Add the ginger, and continue to sauté another minute.

2. Add the curry powder, cayenne, and $1/4$ cup of the water to the pot, and stir well. Cook 1 to 2 minutes.

3. Add the carrots, sweet potato, salt, and the remaining water to the pot, and bring to a boil over high heat. Reduce the heat to low, and simmer 25 to 30 minutes, or until the carrots and sweet potato are soft and tender.

4. Transfer the soup to a blender or food processor, and purée until smooth. (You may have to do this in multiple batches.) Return the puréed soup to the pot, stir in the coconut milk and lime juice, and continue to heat.

5. Serve piping hot.

Cannellini and Pasta Soup

This hearty soup is stick-to-your-ribs satisfying.

Yield: 6 to 8 servings

- 1 tablespoon extra-virgin olive oil
- 1 small fennel bulb, finely chopped
- 1 medium onion, diced
- 2 stalks celery, chopped
- 2 cloves garlic, minced
- 1 teaspoon dried oregano

- 1 tablespoon chopped fresh basil or 1 teaspoon dried
- $1/4$ teaspoon red pepper flakes
- 28-ounce can diced tomatoes, not drained
- 15-ounce can cannellini or other white bean, rinsed and drained

- 6 cups Nanz' Vegetable Stock (page 64), or commercial variety
- 1 teaspoon sea salt
- 8 ounces shell- or elbow-shaped quinoa, rice, or corn pasta
- Chopped fresh parsley for garnish

1. Heat the oil in large pot over medium-low heat. Add the fennel, onion, and celery, and sauté 5 to 7 minutes, or until beginning to soften. Stir the garlic, oregano, basil, and pepper flakes into the pot, and sauté another minute.

2. Add the tomatoes, beans, stock, and salt to the pot, and bring to a boil over high heat. Reduce the heat to low, and simmer 10 to 15 minutes.

3. Stir the pasta into the pot, and cook 10 to 12 minutes or until the pasta is tender.

4. Ladle the piping hot soup into bowls, and sprinkle with parsley before serving.

Curried Chickpea Soup

*The rich earthy flavor of chickpeas pairs perfectly with
spicy curry in this Middle Eastern inspired soup.*

Yield: 5 to 6 servings

1 tablespoon extra-virgin olive oil

1 large yellow onion, finely chopped

1 tablespoon curry powder

1 teaspoon cinnamon (optional)

1 teaspoon ground turmeric

$1/2$ teaspoon chili powder

$1/4$ teaspoon nutmeg

1 cup chopped fresh spinach

15-ounce can chickpeas, rinsed and drained

2 medium tomatoes, chopped

4 cups Nanz' Vegetable Stock (page 64), or commercial variety

13.5-ounce can coconut milk

Chopped fresh parsley for garnish

1. Heat the oil in large pot over medium-low heat. Add the onion, and sauté 2 to 3 minutes or until beginning to soften. Add the curry powder, cinnamon (if using), turmeric, chili powder, and nutmeg. Stir well, add the spinach, and continue to sauté another 2 minutes.

2. Add the chickpeas, tomatoes, stock, and coconut milk to the pot, and bring to a boil over high heat. Reduce the heat to low and simmer 20 to 25 minutes.

3. Ladle the piping hot soup into bowls, garnish with a sprinkling of chopped parsley, and serve.

Spicy Red Lentil Soup

Lentils and quinoa are a delightful duet in this spicy soup.

Yield: 5 to 6 servings

1 tablespoon extra-virgin olive oil

1 large leek, cleaned well and sliced

3 cloves garlic, minced

1 red bell pepper, seeded and diced

2 cups chopped tomatoes

2/3 cup red lentils

1/4 cup quinoa, rinsed and drained

1 teaspoon ground turmeric

1/2 teaspoon chili powder

6 cups Nanz' Vegetable Stock (page 64), commercial stock, or water

1 tablespoon lemon juice

1 teaspoon sea salt

1/4 teaspoon black pepper

1. Heat the oil in a large pot over medium-low heat. Add the leek and garlic, and sauté 2 to 3 minutes or until beginning to soften. Add the bell pepper, tomatoes, lentils, quinoa, turmeric, and chili powder. Stir well.

2. Add the stock to the pot and bring to a boil over high heat. Reduce the heat to low, cover, and simmer 15 to 20 minutes or until the lentils are soft and the quinoa is tender.

3. Stir the lemon juice, salt, and pepper into the soup, and continue to simmer until heated through.

4. Serve piping hot.

Tomato Millet Soup

Millet adds a bit of texture to this flavorful and easy-to-prepare tomato soup.

Yield: 2 to 3 servings

2 tablespoons extra-virgin olive oil

I medium yellow onion, diced

3 cloves garlic, minced

2 medium carrots, diced

28-ounce can crushed tomatoes

1/4 cup chopped fresh basil

I tablespoon dried oregano

I cup cooked millet

1/2 cup rice milk

1. Heat the oil in a large pot over medium-low heat. Add the onion and garlic, and sauté 2 to 3 minutes or until beginning to soften. Add the carrots, and continue to sauté about 3 to 5 minutes or until tender.

2. Add the tomatoes, basil, and oregano to the pot, and bring to boil over high heat. Reduce the heat to low, cover, and simmer 25 to 30 minutes, stirring frequently.

3. Stir the millet and rice milk into the pot, and continue to simmer until the soup is heated through.

4. Serve piping hot.

CHANGE IT UP . . .

• Substitute brown rice, black rice, or quinoa for the millet.

Fiesta Tortilla Soup

This Mexican-inspired soup is hearty and delicious.
The jalapeños add a nice burst of heat. ¡Muy caliente!

Yield: 6 to 8 servings

2 tablespoons extra-virgin olive oil

1 medium yellow onion, diced

4 cloves garlic, minced

1 jalapeño chile, seeded and sliced thinly

1 medium red bell pepper, seeded and diced

6 cups Nanz' Vegetable Stock (page 64), or commercial variety

24-ounce can whole tomatoes, coarsely chopped, not drained

15-ounce can pinto beans, rinsed and drained

1 cup corn kernels

1/2 cup chopped fresh cilantro

1 teaspoon sea salt

2 tablespoons lime juice

1 tablespoon ground cumin

2 cups coarsely crushed corn tortilla chips

1. Heat the oil in a large pot over medium-low heat. Add the onion, garlic, jalapeño, and bell pepper, and sauté 3 to 5 minutes or until beginning to soften.

2. Add the stock, tomatoes, beans, corn, cilantro, and salt to the pot, and bring to a boil over high heat. Reduce the heat to low, stir in the lime juice and cumin, and simmer 10 to 15 minutes.

3. Stir the tortilla chips into the soup, and simmer 3 to 4 minutes. Spoon into bowls and serve immediately.

CHANGE IT UP . . .

- Garnish individual servings with sliced black olives and/or avocado.

- For added crunch, top with some crushed chips before serving.

- For an even spicier version, add a sprinkle or two of red pepper flakes or cayenne pepper.

6

Savory Salads

The salad is among the most versatile of foods. You can enjoy it as an appetizing side dish, a simple snack, or a spectacular main course. In some countries, it's even served at the end of the meal. A salad can range from a bowl of fresh lettuce tossed with a splash of flavorful dressing to an elaborate complete-meal presentation of cooked and/or raw ingredients.

In this chapter, we have shared a number of our favorite, most-requested salads. With the exception of the Seaside Caesar Salad, most of our choices veer from the fresh green varieties, and focus more on salads made with products like brown rice, quinoa, beans, and fresh fruits and vegetables. All are delicious, nutritious, and sure to satisfy.

If you're in the mood for something simple and refreshing with lots of crunch, be sure to try the Marinated Cucumber Slices with Dill or the Gingery Carrot Salad. The Asian-inspired Jicama Slaw is another great choice (as are all of the slaws in this chapter). When something heartier

is what you're craving, you'll find plenty of recipes to fill the bill. There's a Hearty Rice and Bean Salad that's bursting with flavor, a Festive Fiesta Rice Salad that's as visually appealing as it is delicious, and an exotic Black Rice and Mango Salad that never fails to garner high praise.

We've also included a parade of delectable vegetable salads that spotlight ingredients like beets and broccoli and green beans. Our chilled pasta salad, made with rice penne, is a summertime favorite that's always a hit. And quinoa replaces the traditional bulgur wheat in our sensational gluten-free tabouli, which easily rivals the classic Middle-Eastern version. Rounding out this chapter are a number of easy-to-make dressings and vinaigrettes, as well as instructions for making your own homemade mayonnaise.

So whether you're in the mood for a light snack, a substantial side, or a hearty meal, you'll find the salad you're looking for on the following pages. Enjoy!

Lemony Chickpea Salad

Fresh tomatoes, crunchy bell peppers, and bits of red onion are tossed with chickpeas in this lemony-good salad.

Yield: 2 servings

1/4 cup extra-virgin olive oil

2 tablespoons lemon juice

1/4 teaspoon sea salt

1/4 teaspoon black pepper

15-ounce can chickpeas, rinsed and drained

1/2 small red onion, diced

1/4 cup diced red bell pepper

1 small clove garlic, minced

1 large tomato, diced

2 tablespoons finely chopped fresh parsley

1. Whisk together the oil, lemon juice, salt, and pepper in a medium bowl.

2. Add all of the remaining ingredients to the bowl and toss well.

3. Cover and refrigerate at least 1 hour. Serve chilled.

CHANGE IT UP . . .

- For a different taste, replace the lemon juice with lime juice or red wine vinegar.

Chickpea-Tomato Salad with Fresh Basil

*Marinating really brings out the flavors
in this delicious chickpea salad.*

Yield: 2 servings

2 tablespoons extra-virgin olive oil

1 tablespoon lemon juice

1 tablespoon apple cider vinegar

1 tablespoon chopped fresh parsley or 1 teaspoon dried

1/2 teaspoon black pepper

1/4 teaspoon sea salt

15-ounce can chickpeas, rinsed and drained

1 large tomato, diced

1 small red onion, diced

1 clove garlic, minced

1/2 cup chopped fresh basil

1. Whisk together the oil, lemon juice, vinegar, parsley, pepper, and salt in a medium bowl.

2. Add all of the remaining ingredients to the bowl and toss well.

3. Cover and refrigerate at least 1 hour. Serve chilled.

CHANGE IT UP . . .

- Toss 1/2 cup sliced black olives with the ingredients in Step 2.

- For a touch of sweetness, add a teaspoon of honey or agave nectar to the dressing in Step 1.

- Try this salad with kidney beans instead of chickpeas.

Hearty
Rice and Bean Salad

This savory rice and bean salad is bursting with flavor.

Yield: 4 servings

2 tablespoons extra-virgin olive oil

2 tablespoons apple cider vinegar

1 teaspoon hot sauce

1 clove garlic, minced

1 teaspoon dried marjoram

1 teaspoon dried thyme

15-ounce can kidney beans, rinsed and drained

2 cups cooked brown rice

2 large tomatoes, diced

1 cup sliced black olives

2 scallions, thinly sliced

1 large stalk celery, diced

1. Whisk together the oil, vinegar, hot sauce, garlic, marjoram, and thyme in a medium bowl.

2. Add all of the remaining ingredients to the bowl and toss well.

3. Serve immediately or refrigerate and enjoy chilled.

Curried Brown Rice and Grape Salad

Sweet grapes add the perfect balance to curry-flavored rice in this salad.

1. Whisk together the lemon juice, oil, curry powder, and pepper in a medium bowl.

2. Add all of the remaining ingredients to the bowl and toss well.

3. Serve immediately or refrigerate and enjoy chilled.

Yield: 2 servings

1/4 cup lemon juice

1/4 cup extra-virgin olive oil

1 teaspoon curry powder

1/4 teaspoon black pepper

2 cups cooked brown rice

1 cup chopped celery

1 cup halved seedless grapes

1/2 cup thinly sliced scallions

Cherry Tomato and Olive Salad

Toasted sunflower seeds add a bit of crunch to this sweet, colorful tomato salad.

1. Whisk together the oil, vinegar, garlic, basil, and salt in a medium bowl.

2. Add all of the remaining ingredients to the bowl and toss well.

3. Serve immediately or refrigerate and serve chilled.

Yield: 4 servings

1/2 cup extra-virgin olive oil

1/4 cup red wine vinegar

2 cloves garlic, minced

1 tablespoon chopped fresh basil, or 1 teaspoon dried

1 teaspoon sea salt

3 cups halved cherry tomatoes

1 cup pitted black olives

4 scallions, chopped

1/2 cup toasted sunflower seeds

Black-Eyed Peas, Tomato, and Parsley Salad

Black-eyed peas are spotlighted in this fresh, flavorful, fiber-rich salad.

Yield: 4 servings

. . . .

$^1/_4$ cup lemon juice

$^1/_4$ cup extra-virgin olive oil

I teaspoon Dijon-style mustard

2 cloves garlic, minced

$^1/_2$ teaspoon sea salt

$^1/_2$ teaspoon black pepper

2 cans (15-ounces each) black eyed peas, rinsed and drained

I small red onion, quartered and thinly sliced

I cup halved cherry or grape tomatoes

$^3/_4$ cup coarsely chopped fresh parsley

Parsley sprigs for garnish

1. Whisk together the lemon juice, oil, mustard, garlic, salt, and pepper in a medium bowl.

2. Add the black-eyed peas, onion, tomatoes, and chopped parsley to the bowl, and toss well.

3. Refrigerate at least 1 hour or until chilled. Serve with a garnish of parsley sprigs.

Southwest Black Bean Salad

Nothing says "southwest" better than the taste of fresh cilantro and black beans.

Yield: 4 servings

$1/4$ cup extra-virgin olive oil

$1/4$ cup lime juice

$1/2$ teaspoon sea salt

$1/8$ teaspoon black pepper

$1/4$ cup chopped fresh cilantro

15-ounce can black beans, rinsed and drained

2 cups cooked corn kernels

1 medium tomato, diced

1 cup shredded red cabbage

1 small red onion, diced

$1/2$ cup sliced black olives

1. Whisk together the oil, lime juice, salt, and pepper in a medium bowl. Stir in the cilantro.

2. Add all of the remaining ingredients to the bowl and toss well.

3. Serve immediately or refrigerate and enjoy chilled.

CHANGE IT UP . . .

- For added crunch, toss in $1/2$ cup toasted sunflower seeds to the mixture.

- Include a diced avocado for added flavor and creamy texture.

Black Rice and Mango Salad

*Black rice—also known as Chinese "forbidden" black rice—
has a delicious nutty flavor and turns a beautiful deep purple color
when cooked. Tossing it with golden chunks of luscious mango
results in a dish that is as visually appealing as it is delicious.*

Yield: 3 servings

1 cup black rice

2 cups water

2 cups diced mango

1/2 cup thinly sliced scallions

1/4 cup finely chopped fresh parsley

2 tablespoons finely chopped fresh cilantro

2 tablespoons finely chopped fresh mint

1/4 cup extra-virgin olive oil

1/2 cup raisins

1. Bring the water to boil in a medium pot. Add the rice, stir once, and reduce the heat to low. Cover and simmer 30 to 35 minutes or until the rice is tender and most of the water is absorbed. Transfer the rice to a large bowl and let cool.

2. Add all of the remaining ingredients to the cooled rice. Stir until well combined.

3. Serve immediately or refrigerate and enjoy chilled.

CHANGE IT UP . . .

- You can use any medium- or long-grain rice variety for this dish (although black rice is visually the most appealing). Quinoa also works well.

Festive Fiesta Rice Salad

This south-of-the-border-inspired salad is flecked with an array of colorful ingredients—very festive!

Yield: 2 servings

- 2 tablespoons extra-virgin olive oil
- 2 tablespoons lemon juice
- 2 cloves garlic, minced
- 1 jalapeño chile, seeded and finely chopped

- $1/2$ teaspoon sea salt
- 2 cups cooked brown rice
- $1/2$ cup cooked corn kernels
- 1 medium tomato, diced
- 1 small red onion, diced

- 1 medium red bell pepper, seeded and diced
- 1 avocado, diced
- 1 celery stalk, finely chopped
- 2 tablespoons finely chopped fresh cilantro

1. Whisk together the oil, lemon juice, garlic, jalapeño chile, and salt in a medium bowl.

2. Add all of the remaining ingredients to the bowl and toss well.

3. Serve immediately or refrigerate and enjoy chilled.

CHANGE IT UP . . .

- For extra heat, add some red pepper flakes in Step 1.
- Try this with quinoa instead of rice.

Perfect Penne Pasta Salad

On hot summer days, this salad is a great choice.
Enjoy it as is or served over a bed of crisp salad greens.

Yield: 4 servings

1 pound penne, shells, or other short rice pasta

1/3 cup apple cider vinegar

1/4 cup extra-virgin olive oil

2 cloves garlic, minced

1 cup halved cherry tomatoes

1 cup frozen peas, thawed

1/2 cup sliced black olives

2 tablespoons chopped fresh basil, or 2 teaspoons dried

1 teaspoon black pepper

1 teaspoon sea salt

1. Cook the pasta according to the package directions. Drain well, place in a large bowl, and let cool.

2. Whisk together the vinegar, oil, and garlic. Add it to the pasta along with the remaining ingredients. Toss together well.

3. Cover and refrigerate at least 2 hours before serving.

Quinoa Tabouli

Traditionally made with bulgur wheat, tabouli is a classic Middle-Eastern salad. This delicious gluten-free version is made with quinoa.

Yield: 4 servings

1 cup quinoa, rinsed

2 cups water

1/4 cup extra-virgin olive oil

1/4 cup lemon juice

2 cloves garlic, minced

3 medium red tomatoes, diced

1 large cucumber, peeled and diced

2 medium scallions, thinly sliced

1/2 cup finely chopped fresh parsley

1/2 cup finely chopped fresh mint

1. Bring the quinoa and water to boil in a medium pot. Reduce the heat to low, cover, and simmer 12 to 15 minutes or until the water is absorbed and the quinoa is tender. Remove from the heat, fluff with a fork, and let cool to room temperature.

2. Whisk together the oil, lemon juice, and garlic in a large bowl. Add the tomatoes, cucumber, scallions, parsley, and mint, and stir well.

3. Add the cooled quinoa to the bowl and toss to coat.

4. Serve immediately or refrigerate and enjoy chilled.

Colorful Cabbage Salad with Orange Vinaigrette

The dressing adds just the right amount of sweetness to this crunchy, very colorful salad.

Yield: 4 servings

2 cups shredded white cabbage

1 cup shredded red cabbage

1 1/2 cups shredded carrots

1/4 cup diced red bell pepper

1/4 cup raisins

DRESSING

2 1/2 cups orange juice

3/4 cup extra-virgin olive oil

1 tablespoon Dijon-style mustard

1 tablespoon minced fresh ginger

1/2 teaspoon black pepper

1. Whisk together all of the dressing ingredients and set aside.

2. Place the cabbage, carrots, bell pepper, and raisins in a large bowl. Add the dressing and toss well.

3. Cover and refrigerate at least 1 hour. Serve chilled.

Jicama Slaw

This Asian-style jicama slaw makes a delicious side dish or light snack.

Yield: 2 servings

1/4 cup lime juice

2 tablespoons sesame oil

1 tablespoon honey

2 cups shredded jicama

1/2 cup finely chopped or grated red onion

2 tablespoons sesame seeds

1. Whisk together the lime juice, sesame oil, and honey in a medium bowl.

2. Add the jicama and onion to the bowl and toss well.

3. Sprinkle with sesame seeds and serve immediately, or refrigerate and enjoy chilled.

Creamy Coleslaw

*This creamy coleslaw calls for vegan mayonnaise.
We recommend Follow Your Heart brand
Soy-Free Vegenaise Dressing and Sandwich Spread.
Of course, you can also use your own homemade variety
(see the recipes on pages 100 and 101).*

Yield: 6 servings

2 cups shredded green cabbage

2 cups shredded purple cabbage

1 cup shredded carrots

1 medium red onion, finely chopped

3 stalks celery, finely chopped

$3/4$ cup soy-free vegan mayonnaise

$1/3$ cup fresh lemon juice

3 tablespoons pure maple syrup or agave nectar

1 teaspoon celery seeds

1 teaspoon black pepper

1. Place the green cabbage, purple cabbage, carrots, onion, and celery in a large mixing bowl.

2. Add all of the remaining ingredients to the bowl and stir until well coated.

3. Cover and refrigerate at least three hours (the longer it sits, the more flavorful it becomes). Serve chilled. Refrigerate leftovers up to one week.

CHANGE IT UP . . .

• For an added touch of sweetness, color, and texture, stir a handful of cooked corn kernels and/or cranberries (fresh or dried) into the slaw.

MMMM . . .

Mayonnaise is so versatile. You can use it as a sandwich spread, a flavorful addition to salads, or even as a creamy dipping sauce for French fries, chips, and crisp raw veggies.

When it comes to commercial mayonnaise, we recommend Follow Your Heart brand Soy-Free Vegenaise Dressing and Sandwich Spread. It's smooth, creamy, and tastes delicious. But if you would like to try making your own, here are two recipes that are prepared in a

Creamy Mayonnaise I

Yield: About I cup

$^1/_3$ cup cold rice milk

I tablespoon lemon juice

$^1/_8$ teaspoon white pepper

$^1/_2$ teaspoon xanthan gum*

$^1/_4$ cup plus 2 tablespoons extra-virgin olive oil

$^1/_4$ cup plus 2 tablespoons safflower oil

$^1/_2$ teaspoon finely ground sea salt, or to taste

I small clove garlic, minced (optional)

1. Place the rice milk, lemon juice, pepper, and xanthan gum in a blender. Blend on high speed about 1 minute or until foamy.

2. With the blender running on high speed, slowly add the oil one drop at a time through the opening in the lid. Continue for 5 minutes, or until about the half the oil has been added and the mixture begins to emulsify. At this point, you can begin to add the remaining oil in a very thin steady drip. Keep mixing until the mayonnaise is smooth and creamy. (It will be more liquidy than thick.) Add the salt and garlic (if using) and stir well.

3. Transfer the mayonnaise to an airtight container and refrigerate up to a week.

* Used as a thickening agent, xanthan gum is available in most natural foods stores.

. . . MAYONNAISE

blender. Just be aware that both recipes require time and patience—adding the oil must be done very, very slowly in order for the mixture to emulsify properly. We recommend using a condiment squeeze bottle or an eye-dropper for this. For both recipes, it will take anywhere from 10 to 15 minutes to add the oil. For this reason, you may want to turn off the blender every few minutes to let the motor rest. Use this time to scrape down the sides of the blender.

Creamy Mayonnaise II

1. Place all the ingredients except the oil in a bowl and whisk until well blended. Transfer to a blender.

2. With the blender running on high speed, slowly add the oil one drop at a time through the opening in the lid. Continue for 5 minutes, or until about the half the oil has been added and the mixture begins to emulsify. At this point, you can begin to add the remaining oil in a very thin steady drip. Keep mixing until the mayonnaise is thick and creamy.

3. Transfer the mayonnaise to an airtight container and refrigerate up to a week.

Yield: About 1 cup

1 egg made with Ener-G Egg Replacer

1 tablespoon vinegar (rice, apple, and white wine are recommended)

1 teaspoon lemon juice

1 teaspoon agave nectar

1 small clove garlic, minced (optional)

$1/2$ teaspoon finely ground sea salt, or to taste

$1/4$ teaspoon dry mustard

1 cup safflower oil

Carrot-Apple Slaw

Colorful and tasty!

Yield: 4 servings

. . . .

$1/2$ cup orange juice

$1/4$ cup sunflower oil

3 tablespoons chopped
fresh cilantro

$1/2$ teaspoon black pepper

4 large carrots, grated

1 Granny Smith apple,
unpeeled and grated

1 red onion, finely chopped

$1/2$ cup dried cranberries

$1/2$ cup toasted pumpkin seeds

1. Whisk together the orange juice, oil, cilantro, and pepper in medium bowl.

2. Add all of the remaining ingredients to the bowl and toss well.

3. Serve immediately or refrigerate and enjoy chilled.

CHANGE IT UP . . .

• For an Asian flair, replace the sunflower oil with 2 or 3 tablespoons of sesame oil.

Four-Berry Sun Salad

This very-berry salad also makes a delicious anytime snack.

Yield: 4 servings

. . . .

2 cups strawberries

1 cup blueberries

1 cup raspberries

$1/2$ cup blackberries

2 tablespoons balsamic
vinegar

2 tablespoons pure
maple syrup

$1/4$ cup toasted sunflower
seeds for garnish

1. Place the strawberries, blueberries, raspberries, and blackberries in a large bowl.

2. Whisk together the vinegar and maple syrup. Pour over the berries and toss well.

3. Sprinkle with sunflower seeds before serving.

CHANGE IT UP . . .

- Add a tablespoon of poppy seeds to the sunflower seeds before garnishing this salad.

- Instead of sunflower seeds, garnish this salad with crispy rice cereal or Great Gluten-Free Granola (page 165).

Jicama Salad With Mango

Crunchy cubes of jicama and bits of cucumber are tossed with sweet juicy mango in this refreshing summertime salad.

Yield: 2 servings

$^1/_2$ cup brown rice vinegar	1 large cucumber, peeled and diced	1 cup cubed mango ($^1/_2$-inch cubes)
$^1/_2$ cup water	1 cup cubed jicama ($^1/_2$-inch cubes)	2 tablespoons coarsely chopped fresh mint
2 tablespoons agave nectar		
2 tablespoons lime juice		

1. Place the vinegar, water, agave, and lime juice in a small pot over medium heat. Simmer for 2 minutes or until the liquid is clear and slightly thick. Remove from the heat and let cool at least 15 minutes.

2. Place the cucumber, jicama, and mango in a medium bowl. Add the cooled vinegar mixture and mint, and toss well.

3. Serve immediately or refrigerate and serve chilled.

Gingery Carrot Salad

*Sesame seeds add extra crunch
to this Asian-inspired carrot salad.*

Yield: 1 to 2 servings

1/4 cup toasted sesame oil

2 tablespoons rice vinegar

2 tablespoons tahini
(sesame seed butter)

1 tablespoon grated fresh ginger

1/2 teaspoon black pepper

4 large carrots, grated

2 tablespoons sesame seeds

2 tablespoons chopped
fresh parsley

1. Whisk together the sesame oil, rice vinegar, tahini, ginger, and pepper in a small bowl.

2. Place the carrots, sesame seeds, and parsley in a medium bowl. Add the dressing and toss well.

3. Serve immediately or refrigerate and serve chilled.

Grapefruit Salad With Avocado and Arugula

*Juicy grapefruit balances the peppery arugula
in this salad. Avocado adds rich creaminess.*

Yield: 4 servings

2 medium grapefruits

2 tablespoons agave nectar

2 tablespoons fresh lime juice

3 cups arugula leaves

1 Hass avocado, diced

1/4 cup toasted pumpkin seeds

1. Peel the grapefruits, separate the sections, and cut in half.

2. Place the agave and lime juice in a medium bowl and stir until well blended. Add the arugula, grapefruit, and avocado. Toss well.

3. Sprinkle with pumpkin seeds before serving.

CHANGE IT UP . . .

- Add $1/2$ cup sliced fresh strawberries or blueberries to this salad.
- For a heartier version, toss the ingredients with a cup of cooled cooked rice or quinoa.

coleslaw with Lemon-Cilantro Vinaigrette

This tasty coleslaw is a light alternative to the traditional mayonnaise and sugar-laced version.

Yield: 4 to 6 servings

1 medium green cabbage, shredded

1 medium yellow onion, finely chopped

2 large carrots, grated

VINAIGRETTE

$1/4$ cup lemon juice

2 tablespoons agave nectar or pure maple syrup

1 tablespoon finely chopped fresh cilantro

1 tablespoon Dijon-style mustard

$2/3$ cup extra-virgin olive oil

1. Place all of the vinaigrette ingredients except the olive oil in a blender, and blend for 10 to 15 seconds. Slowly add the oil, and continue to blend until smooth.

2. Place the cabbage, onion, and carrots in a large bowl. Add the vinaigrette and toss well.

3. Refrigerate and serve chilled. Store leftovers in the refrigerator up to a week.

Moroccan Beet Salad

Yield: 3 servings

4 large beets, scrubbed well

1 medium red onion, thinly sliced

6 tablespoons extra-virgin olive oil

3 tablespoons lemon juice

2 cloves garlic, minced

3/4 teaspoon ground cumin

1/4 teaspoon sea salt

1/8 teaspoon black pepper

This salad is best serve chilled, either alone or over a bed of greens. Also delicious on top of freshly cooked quinoa or brown rice.

1. Bring the beets to boil in a pot of water over medium-high heat. Reduce the heat to medium, cover, and cook for 40 to 45 minutes or until the beets are tender when pierced with a fork. Remove the beets, and let sit until cool enough to handle. Peel and discard the skins.

2. Cut the beets into bite-sized pieces, and place in a medium bowl along with the onion.

3. Whisk together all of the remaining ingredients. Pour over the beets and toss well.

4. Refrigerate at least two hours. Serve chilled.

Broccoli Floret Salad

Yield: 6 servings

2 large bunches broccoli

1/3 cup brown rice vinegar

1/3 cup extra-virgin olive oil

3 tablespoons honey

1 teaspoon garlic powder

1 teaspoon sea salt

1 teaspoon black pepper

1/2 cup raisins

2 tablespoons toasted sunflower seeds

Even non-broccoli fans will enjoy this nutritious raw salad.

1. Separate the broccoli into bite-sized florets, and place in a large bowl.

2. Whisk together the vinegar, oil, honey, garlic powder, salt, and pepper. Pour over the florets and toss well.

3. Add the raisins and sunflower seeds, and continue to toss.

4. Serve immediately or refrigerate and serve chilled. Refrigerate leftovers up to four days.

CHANGE IT UP . . .

- Instead of raw broccoli, try this salad with cooked or blanched florets.

- For a vegan version, use agave nectar instead of honey.

- If tree nuts are not an allergy concern, try substituting $1/4$ cup slivered almonds for the sunflower seeds.

Kale-Veggie Salad with Lemon-Tahini Dressing

Tahini—sesame seed butter—is the main dressing ingredient for this salad. Those who are sesame sensitive can use sunflower butter instead with equally delicious results. We also enjoy this dressing as a luscious dip for raw veggies and gluten-free chips.

1. Place the kale, carrots, avocado, onion, and celery in a large bowl.

2. Blend all of the dressing ingredients in a food processor or blender until smooth. Pour over the vegetables and toss well.

3. Sprinkle with toasted pumpkin seeds before serving.

Yield: 4 servings

8 cups chopped kale

2 cups grated carrots

2 avocados, diced

I medium red onion, diced

2 celery stalks, diced

$1/2$ cup toasted pumpkin seeds for garnish

DRESSING

$3/4$ cup tahini (sesame seed butter)

$1/3$ cup lemon juice

$1/2$ cup extra-virgin olive oil

$1/4$ cup soy-free soy sauce*

$1/4$ cup chopped green bell pepper

I stalk celery, chopped

I medium yellow onion, chopped

3 cloves garlic, quartered

*We recommend coconut aminos (see page 145).

Marinated Cucumber Slices With Dill

Yield: 2 servings

¼ cup apple cider vinegar

1 tablespoon chopped fresh dill, or 1 teaspoon dried

¼ teaspoon black pepper

1 large cucumber, sliced into rounds

This simple refreshing side dish also makes a great summertime snack.

1. Place the vinegar, dill, and pepper in small shallow bowl and mix well. Add the cucumber slices and toss to coat.

2. Refrigerate at least 1 hour. Serve chilled.

Green Beans and Scallions

Yield: 4 servings

1 pound fresh green beans, cut into bite-sized pieces

6 scallions, finely chopped

¼ cup apple cider vinegar

¼ cup extra-virgin olive oil

2 cloves garlic, minced

1 tablespoon chopped fresh basil, or 1 teaspoon dried

½ teaspoon sea salt

½ teaspoon black pepper

Another summertime favorite, this salad gets its wonderful crunch from raw green beans.

1. Place the green beans and scallions in a large bowl.

2. Whisk together all of the remaining ingredients. Pour over the beans and scallions, and toss well.

3. Serve immediately or refrigerate and enjoy chilled.

CHANGE IT UP . . .

- Try this salad with cooked or blanched green beans instead of raw.

Green Bean and Tomato Salad

This green bean salad is rich with sweet cherry tomatoes and slices of red onion.

Yield: 6 servings

2 pounds green beans

1 1/2 teaspoons Dijon-style mustard

2 tablespoons red wine vinegar

5 tablespoons extra-virgin olive oil

1/2 teaspoon sea salt

1 cup halved cherry tomatoes

1 medium red onion, thinly sliced

1 tablespoon chopped fresh tarragon, or 1 teaspoon dried

2 teaspoons chopped fresh thyme, or 1/2 teaspoon dried

1. Bring a large pot of water to a boil. Add the beans and cook for 4 to 5 minutes, or until bright green and tender-crisp. Drain, rinse under cold water, and pat dry.

2. Whisk together the mustard and vinegar in a large bowl. Add the olive oil and salt, and continue to whisk until well blended.

3. Add the beans and all of the remaining ingredients to the bowl, and toss until well coated.

4. Serve immediately, or refrigerate and enjoy chilled.

Sweet Potato Salad with Chipotle Vinaigrette

Here's a sweet potato salad that's full of flavor. Chipotle chiles add smoky heat to the vinaigrette.

Yield: 6 to 8 servings

3 pounds sweet potatoes, peeled and cut into $1/4$-inch-thick rounds

$1/4$ cup extra-virgin olive oil

$1/8$ teaspoon black pepper

$1/2$ teaspoon sea salt

6 scallions, sliced

$1/2$ cup raisins

$1/2$ cup toasted sunflower seeds

VINAIGRETTE

$1 1/2$ cups extra-virgin olive oil

$1/2$ cup lime juice

$1/4$ cup balsamic vinegar

2 tablespoons honey or agave nectar

6-ounce can chipotle chiles

2 shallots, finely chopped

1. Preheat the oven to 375°F.

2. Place the potato slices in a large bowl. Add the olive oil, salt, and pepper, and toss to coat.

3. Arrange the slices on a baking sheet. Bake for 15 to 20 minutes or until tender. Remove from the oven and let cool to room temperature.

4. To prepare the vinaigrette, whisk together the olive oil, lime juice, vinegar, and honey in a large bowl. Add the chipotle and shallots, and continue to whisk until well blended.

5. Add the potatoes, scallions, and raisins to the bowl, and stir until well coated with the dressing. Transfer to a shallow serving bowl, sprinkle with sunflower seeds, and serve.

CHANGE IT UP . . .

- If nuts are not an allergy concern, try substituting the sunflower seeds with pecans.

QUICK-AND-EASY SALAD DRESSINGS

The right dressing can make an otherwise "ho-hum" bed of greens really spring to life. Here we have shared two of our tried-and-true favorites. Along with adding them to fresh green salads, we enjoy them as dips for raw veggies, crackers, and chips. We also drizzle them on grain or bean burgers for an added burst of flavor, and add a spoonful or two to many cooked vegetables and simple sides like brown rice, quinoa, and lentils.

We prefer using apple cider vinegar in our dressings and marinades, but feel free to use any type of vinegar you prefer. And substitute flaxseed, grapeseed, safflower, or sunflower oil for the olive oil.

We hope you enjoy our "classic" dressings as much as we do.

Garlic-Herb Vinaigrette

1. Place the vinegar, mustard, garlic, salt, thyme, and basil in a clean glass jar. Cover the jar and shake well.

2. Add the oil and water to the jar, cover, and continue to shake until well blended.

3. Use immediately, or refrigerate up to two weeks.

Yield: About 2 cups

. . . .

$3/4$ cup apple cider vinegar

1 tablespoon Dijon-style mustard

4 cloves garlic, minced

$1/2$ teaspoon sea salt

2 teaspoons chopped fresh thyme

2 teaspoons fresh chopped basil

$1 1/2$ cups extra-virgin olive oil

1 tablespoon water

Lemon Vinaigrette

1. Place all of the ingredients in a clean glass jar. Cover the jar and shake well.

2. Use immediately, or refrigerate up to two weeks.

Yield: About 2 cups

. . . .

1 cup lemon juice

1 cup extra-virgin olive oil

2 cloves garlic, minced

1 teaspoon paprika

1 teaspoon sea salt

Seaside Caesar Salad

In our homes, this tasty (anchovy-free) Caesar salad is an all-time family favorite.

Yield: 3 servings

I large head romaine lettuce

I large tomato, chopped

$1/4$ cup extra-virgin olive oil

2 tablespoons lemon juice

2 cloves garlic, minced

$1/2$ teaspoon sea salt

$1/2$ teaspoon black pepper

$1/4$ cup grated vegan Parmesan

I cup Crunchy Croutons (page 57), or other gluten-free variety

1. Separate the lettuce leaves, rinse well, and pat dry. Tear into bite-sized pieces and place in a large bowl along with the tomato.

2. Whisk together the olive oil, lemon juice, garlic, salt, and pepper. Pour over the lettuce, add the Parmesan and croutons, and toss well. Serve immediately.

CHANGE IT UP . . .

- For a milder-tasting version, use shredded vegan mozzarella instead of Parmesan.

- If nuts are not an allergy concern, try adding a handful of pine nuts to the salad.

7

Sensational Sides

While main dishes are typically the mealtime "stars," side dishes can be just as impressive, and the recipes we have selected for this chapter are among our most inspired. They are family favorites—ones we have prepared often over the years.

Potatoes are always a hit, and we have shared a number of recipes that place them in the spotlight. There are a few classic choices like light and fluffy Mashed Potatoes and oven-baked Sweet Potato Fries that are enjoyed by kids of all ages! Then there are our Potato Latkes—onion-flecked pancakes that are crispy and browned on the outside, while soft and tender on the inside. You and your family will love every bite! And whether you serve our super flavorful Garlicky Potato-Mushroom Medley hot from the oven, chilled, or at room temperature, it's always a welcomed dish.

While the Green Bean Casserole, Honey-Kissed Carrots, and Maple-Roasted Butternut Squash with Currants are among our traditional Thanksgiving favorites, we also find ourselves making them often throughout the year. Our families also put in regular requests for the savory Cauliflower Bakes—fresh cauliflower florets that are tossed in a garlicky lemon-mustard sauce and then baked to perfection. It seems that no matter how many we make, they're gone in a wink!

If you like the flavor of salty sweetness, you're going to love our Roasted Brussels Sprouts. The halved sprouts are tossed with a blend of Dijon-style mustard and pure maple syrup, and then oven-roasted until browned and tender. Absolutely delicious! And be sure to try the chilled Tangy Orange-Laced Soba Noodles and the colorful Quinoa Confetti as lunchtime entrées as well as super sides.

Once you've tried the side dishes in this chapter, we're betting you'll be making them a regular part of your family's healthy allergen-free diet. Easy-to-prepare, nutritious, and delicious!

Chilled Asparagus With Fresh Basil

This dish is a springtime favorite,
when asparagus is at its peak of flavor and freshness.

Yield: 3 servings

- 1 pound asparagus, diagonally cut into $1/2$-inch pieces
- 2 tablespoons sesame oil
- 2 tablespoons apple cider vinegar
- 1 tablespoon agave nectar or pure maple syrup (optional)
- $1/2$ teaspoon dried Italian seasoning blend
- $1/2$ cup chopped fresh basil
- 2 tablespoons toasted sesame seeds for garnish

1. Bring a medium pot of water to boil, add the asparagus, and cook for 2 minutes or until bright green and tender-crisp. Drain, rinse under cold water, and pat dry. Place in a medium bowl.

2. Whisk together the sesame oil, vinegar, agave nectar (if using), and seasoning blend in a small bowl. Add the basil and stir well.

3. Pour the dressing over the asparagus and toss to coat.

4. Refrigerate at least 1 hour or until chilled.

5. Garnish with sesame seeds before serving.

Tangy Orange-Laced Soba Noodles

Try these flavorful noodles cold as a satisfying lunch-time entrée.

Yield: 4 servings

8 ounces buckwheat
noodles (soba)

1/4 cup extra-virgin
olive oil

1/4 cup balsamic vinegar

1/3 cup orange juice

2 cloves garlic, minced

2 teaspoons crushed anise
seeds (optional)

1/4 teaspoon black pepper

1/4 teaspoon cinnamon

2 oranges, sectioned
and chopped

1 small red onion,
chopped

1. Bring a pot of water to boil. Add the soba noodles, and cook about 5 minutes or until tender and somewhat chewy. Drain well and place in a large bowl.

2. Whisk together the olive oil, vinegar, orange juice, garlic, anise seeds (if using), pepper, and cinnamon in a medium bowl. Add the oranges and onions, and stir well. Pour the mixture over the soba noodles and toss to coat.

3. Serve immediately, or refrigerate and enjoy chilled.

CHANGE IT UP . . .

- For added taste and texture, add 1/4 cup toasted sesame seeds or raisins to the dressing.

Green Bean Casserole

Although this dish is a traditional holiday hit, you can enjoy it all year round. For convenience, this version calls for canned green beans, but feel free to use frozen (thawed) or freshly cooked. For a mild cheesy flavor, include the nutritional yeast.

Yield: 4 servings

1/4 cup extra-virgin olive oil

1/4 cup brown rice flour

1 1/2 cups Nanz' Vegetable Stock (page 64), or commercial variety

1 teaspoon sea salt

1/2 teaspoon garlic powder

1/4 cup nutritional yeast (optional)

2 cans (14.5-ounces each) regular or French-style green beans, drained

2.8-ounce can gluten-free French fried onions

1. Preheat the oven to 350°F. Lightly oil a 2-quart casserole dish and set aside.

2. Heat the oil in a medium pot over low heat. Add the flour and whisk continuously for about 2 minutes. Add the stock, salt, and garlic powder, and continue to whisk another 1 or 2 minutes or until the sauce is thick and bubbly. Stir in the nutritional yeast (if using).

3. Pour the sauce into the prepared casserole dish, add the green beans, and stir to coat.

4. Bake for 10 minutes, then top with the onions. Continue to bake another 10 minutes or until browned and bubbly. Serve piping hot.

NUTRITIONAL YEAST

Not to be confused with brewer's yeast, torula yeast, dry active yeast, or fresh cake yeast, nutritional yeast is a food supplement that is very rich in protein and B vitamins. It comes in thin golden flakes that add a rich, slightly cheesy flavor to many foods, including soups, spreads, veggie burgers, pizza, and even popcorn! Start with a small amount—a teaspoon or so—then add more to taste.

Honey-Kissed Carrots

Cooking carrots brings out their natural sweetness.
Adding a touch of honey enhances their flavor even more.

Yield: 2 servings

1 cup water

2 tablespoons honey

2 cups coarsely chopped carrots

1 teaspoon sea salt

1 tablespoon finely chopped fresh dill, or 1 teaspoon dried

1. Bring the water to boil in a medium pot. Stir in the honey, add the carrots, and reduce the heat to low.

2. Cover the pot, and cook the carrots for 10 minutes or until tender.

3. Drain the carrots and place in a serving bowl. Sprinkle with salt and dill, toss, and serve.

CHANGE IT UP . . .

- For a vegan version, use pure maple syrup instead of honey.

Cauliflower Bakes

*Fresh cauliflower florets are tossed in a garlicky
lemon-mustard sauce and then baked to perfection.*

Yield: 4 servings

I large head cauliflower,
separated into bite-sized florets

4 cloves garlic, minced

2 tablespoons extra-virgin
olive oil

2 tablespoons lemon juice

2 teaspoons Dijon-style
mustard

I teaspoon sea salt

2 tablespoons nutritional yeast
(optional)

1. Preheat the oven to 350°F. Lightly oil a baking sheet or line with parchment paper. Set aside.

2. Whisk together the garlic, oil, lemon juice, mustard, salt, and nutritional yeast (if using) in a large bowl. Add the cauliflower florets and toss to coat.

3. Arrange the florets in a single layer on the baking sheet. Bake for 25 to 30 minutes or until tender and lightly browned, turning once about halfway through.

4. Transfer the florets to a serving bowl (and watch them disappear).

Roasted Brussels Sprouts

*Brussels sprouts have the perfect balance of salty
sweetness in this savory side dish.*

Yield: 4 servings

4 cups Brussels sprouts,
trimmed and halved lengthwise

2 tablespoons olive oil

2 cloves garlic, minced

3 tablespoons agave nectar or
pure maple syrup

2 tablespoons Dijon-style
mustard

$^1/_2$ teaspoon sea salt

$^1/_4$ teaspoon black pepper

1. Preheat the oven to 375°F. Lightly oil a baking sheet or line with parchment paper. Set aside.

2. Place the Brussels sprouts in a medium bowl. Combine all of the remaining ingredients and pour over the sprouts. Toss to coat.

3. Arrange the sprouts in a single layer on the baking sheet. Roast for 30 to 35 minutes or until the sprouts are tender and the outer leaves are crisp and golden brown. Serve hot.

White Beans and Mushrooms With Sage

Fresh sage adds a flavorful twist to mushrooms and creamy white beans in this easy-to-prepare side.

Yield: 2 servings

2 tablespoons extra virgin olive oil

1 cup sliced white button mushrooms

15-ounce can cannellini or Great Northern beans, rinsed and drained

1 cup tomato sauce

3 cloves garlic, minced

1 tablespoon chopped fresh sage

$1/4$ teaspoon black pepper

1. Heat the oil in a medium pot over medium heat. Add the mushrooms and sauté 4 to 5 minutes or until soft.

2. Add all of the remaining ingredients to the pot. Stirring occasionally, cook for 10 to 15 minutes or until heated through.

3. Transfer the mixture to a bowl and serve.

CHANGE IT UP . . .

- Serve with a generous handful of melted vegan mozzarella on top.

- Enjoy this savory blend on top of rice or quinoa pasta, or spoon some over our fluffy Mashed Potatoes (page 120).

Maple-Roasted Butternut Squash With Currants

Pure maple syrup adds a delicious touch of sweetness to roasted cubes of butternut squash.

Yield: 4 servings

1 large butternut squash, peeled and cut into 1-inch cubes

1/4 cup pure maple syrup

3 tablespoons extra-virgin olive oil

1 teaspoon ground cinnamon

1 teaspoon dried thyme

1/2 teaspoon sea salt

1/3 cup dried currants or cranberries

1. Preheat the oven to 350°F. Lightly oil a baking sheet or line with parchment paper. Set aside.

2. Whisk together the maple syrup, oil, cinnamon, thyme, and salt in a large bowl. Add the squash cubes and toss to coat.

3. Arrange the cubes in a single layer on the prepared baking sheet. Roast for 35 to 45 minutes or until tender and lightly browned, turning once about halfway through.

4. Transfer the cubes to a bowl, sprinkle with currants, and serve.

Mashed Potatoes

Skip the butter, but not the flavor. For the creamiest, fluffiest mashed potatoes, we recommend using Yukon gold potatoes, but russets also work well.

Yield: 6 to 8 servings

8 large Yukon gold potatoes, peeled and cut into 1-inch chunks

1 cup rice milk, warmed

1/4 cup extra-virgin olive oil

1 teaspoon garlic powder

1 teaspoon sea salt, or to taste

1/8 teaspoon nutmeg

1. Bring a large pot of water to boil. Carefully add the potatoes, and cook 15 to 20 minutes or until tender. Drain well and return to the pot.

2. Using a potato ricer or large fork, mash the cooked potatoes.

3. Add the warm rice milk to the potatoes along with the remaining ingredients. Stir until well blended.

4. Transfer to a serving bowl. Enjoy piping hot.

Sweet Potato Fries

These luscious fries are loved by kids and adults alike.

Yield: 4 servings

2 pounds sweet potatoes, peeled and cut into long 1/2-inch-thick strips	3 tablespoons extra-virgin olive oil 1 tablespoon honey	1 teaspoon ground cinnamon

1. Preheat the oven to 350°F. Lightly oil a baking sheet or line with parchment paper. Set aside.

2. Whisk together the oil, honey, and cinnamon. Add the potato strips and toss well.

3. Arrange the strips in a single layer on the baking sheet.

4. Bake for 15 to 20 minutes or until tender and beginning to brown.

5. Transfer to a serving platter and enjoy!

CHANGE IT UP . . .

- For a savory version, use red or russet potatoes, omit the honey, and season with garlic salt instead of cinnamon.

Garlicky Potato-Mushroom Medley

Whether served piping hot, chilled, or at room temp,
this garlicky side dish is always welcomed.

Yield: 4 servings

5 tablespoons extra-virgin olive oil, divided

3 large russet potatoes, thinly sliced

4 cloves garlic, minced

2 tablespoons chopped fresh basil, or 2 teaspoons dried

1 teaspoon sea salt

10 medium white button or crimini mushrooms, thinly sliced

1. Preheat the oven to 350°F.

2. Coat the bottom of a 9-inch-square baking dish with 2 tablespoons of the olive oil.

3. Layer the potato slices in the baking dish. Sprinkle with half the garlic, basil, and salt.

4. Layer the mushroom slices on top, and sprinkle with the remaining garlic, basil, and salt. Drizzle with the remaining 3 tablespoons of oil.

5. Bake uncovered for 35 to 40 minutes or until the potatoes and mushrooms are tender. Serve immediately.

CHANGE IT UP . . .

- Instead of slicing and layering the ingredients, cut the potatoes into small bite-sized chunks and halve the mushrooms. Toss them together with the seasonings, and bake as instructed.

Tomato-Stuffed Portobellos

These savory mushroom caps are crowned with a flavorful mound of chopped fresh tomatoes. Delicious!

Yield: 6 servings

- 1 1/2 cups chopped fresh tomatoes
- 4 tablespoons extra-virgin olive oil, divided
- 1 tablespoon finely chopped fresh oregano

- 1/4 teaspoon black pepper
- 4 cloves garlic, minced
- 3 tablespoons lemon juice
- 1 tablespoon balsamic vinegar

- 6 portobello mushroom caps (5 to 6 inches in diameter)
- 1 tablespoon chopped fresh basil

1. Preheat the oven to 350°F.

2. Whisk together 1 tablespoon of the olive oil, the oregano, black pepper, and garlic in a small bowl. Add the tomatoes and toss to coat.

3. In another small bowl, whisk together the lemon juice, vinegar, and remaining 3 tablespoons of olive oil.

4. Using a pastry brush, brush the lemon-oil mixture on both sides of the mushroom caps. Place the caps gill side down on a baking sheet.

5. Bake the caps about 5 minutes or until beginning to soften. Turn over and cook another 5 to 7 minutes or until soft and tender. Fill each cap with the tomato mixture and bake another 3 to 4 minutes or until heated through.

6. Sprinkle with chopped basil before serving.

Quinoa Confetti

Quinoa is flecked with colorful vegetables and herbs in this side dish, which also makes a satisfying entrée.

Yield: 5 to 6 servings

2 cups quinoa, rinsed and drained

4 cups water

2/3 cup sliced black olives

1 cup finely chopped scallions

1/3 cup diced celery

1/3 cup diced red bell pepper

1/4 cup finely chopped parsley

Toasted sunflower seeds for garnish

DRESSING

1/4 cup extra-virgin olive oil

1/4 cup apple cider vinegar

2 cloves garlic, minced

1/2 teaspoon sea salt

1. Bring the quinoa and water to boil in a medium pot over high heat. Reduce the heat to low, cover, and simmer for 20 to 25 minutes, or until the water is absorbed and the quinoa is tender. Remove from the heat, and let sit a few minutes to cool a bit.

2. While the quinoa is cooling, whisk the dressing ingredients together. Set aside.

3. Stir the olives, scallions, celery, bell pepper, and parsley into the warm quinoa. Add the dressing and mix well.

4. Transfer to a serving bowl and garnish with a generous sprinkling of toasted sunflower seeds.

CHANGE IT UP . . .

- For added color and sweet burst of flavor, add a handful of halved cherry tomatoes to the mixture.

Potato Latkes

These crispy pancakes are always a welcomed side dish.
They also make terrific snacks or appetizers. Because
the raw grated potatoes begin to turn dark quickly,
it is best to grate them right before preparing.

Yield: About 10 latkes

2 large russet potatoes, grated (about 1 1/2 cups)

1 small yellow onion, grated

4 tablespoons brown rice flour

1 teaspoon garlic powder

1 teaspoon sea salt

1/8 teaspoon black pepper

2 tablespoons extra-virgin olive oil

1. Place the grated potatoes in a colander and squeeze out as much moisture as possible. Transfer to a large bowl.

2. Add the onion, flour, garlic powder, salt, and pepper to the potatoes and mix well.

3. Heat the oil in a large skillet over medium-high heat.

4. Drop about 3 tablespoons of the potato mixture onto the skillet and spread into a 3-inch round. Fit as many rounds as possible in the skillet. Cook about 3 minutes on each side or until crisp and browned.

5. Place the cooked latkes on paper towels to absorb any excess oil.

6. Serve hot as is, or enjoy with applesauce, vegan sour cream, or vegan ketchup.

8

Delectable Mains

Perhaps one of the most difficult challenges for the allergen-free cook is preparing foods that are safe to eat but still taste good. Another challenge is expanding the selection of food choices—offering a variety of dishes that make mealtime a pleasurable experience. Having food allergies does not mean deprivation, and the recipes in this chapter will prove it. We have included an international parade of culinary delights that are guaranteed to expand your entrée selections in a delectable way.

Among our best all-American choices, you'll find recipes for Mac 'n Cheese (that all-time favorite for kids of all ages), a savory Hearty Vegetable Stew that's even better the next day, and an Easy Pasta Primavera that is bursting with fresh vegetables. Representing the Southwest, there are black bean burgers and sliders, and a hearty chili made with pinto beans and sweet potatoes. Moving South-of the Border, there's a Mexican-inspired Polenta Casserole and a recipe for crunchy tacos that are filled with a luscious blend of fresh corn and black beans.

From Italy, there is Neapolitan Baked Eggplant and a layered Italian Noodle Casserole that is reminiscent of lasagna. And then there is pizza. Do you know anyone who doesn't like it? Just because you or a family member may be gluten intolerant or allergic to wheat, dairy, or soy, there is no reason to be deprived of this universal favorite. We have included an allergen-free/gluten-free Perfect Pizza Crust recipe and a tomato-based Quick 'n Easy Pizza Sauce to serve as a great pizza foundation. There's also an inset that offers a wide assortment of suggested toppings—including some terrific cheeses.

Finally, with the growing popularity of sushi rolls, you'll find a section dedicated entirely to these Japanese favorites—including a recipe for making the perfect sushi rice, and easy-to-follow instructions (with drawings) for forming the rolls.

The recipes in this chapter are designed to help you expand your culinary choices. We hope you enjoy trying them all.

Pinto Bean and Sweet Potato Chili

Top this chili with a handful of vegan cheddar, and serve it with Aztec Corn Cakes (page 58) and Baked Tortilla Chips (page 56).

Yield: 4 servings

4 tablespoons extra-virgin olive oil

1 large sweet potato, peeled and cut into $1/2$-inch cubes

1 large carrot, diced

1 large onion, diced

4 cloves garlic, minced

2 tablespoons chili powder

1 tablespoon ground cumin

1 teaspoon sea salt

1 cup water

2 cans (15 ounces each) pinto beans, rinsed and drained

1 cup chopped tomatoes

1 cup tomato sauce

$1/3$ cup chopped fresh cilantro

$1/4$ cup lemon juice

1. Heat the oil in a medium pot over medium heat. Add the sweet potato, carrot, and onion, and cook for 4 to 5 minutes or until the onion starts to soften. Add the garlic, chili powder, cumin, and salt. Continue to cook while stirring for about a minute.

2. Add the water to the pot, increase the heat, and bring to a boil. Reduce the heat to medium-low, cover, and gently simmer for 10 to 15 minutes or until the sweet potato is tender.

3. Add all of the remaining ingredients to the pot, and simmer another 10 to 15 minutes.

4. Ladle the hot chili into bowls and serve.

CHANGE IT UP . . .

- Instead of or in combination with pinto beans, try other red bean varieties or black beans.

Bell Pepper and Black Bean Sliders

Cumin adds nutty, peppery flavor to these savory mini burgers. The mixture can be premade and stored in the refrigerator up to twenty-four hours.

Yield: 4 sliders

1 tablespoon extra-virgin olive oil	$1/4$ cup diced red bell pepper	$1/4$ cup oat flour
6 scallions, sliced	1 stalk celery, chopped	1 tablespoon chopped fresh cilantro
2 cloves garlic, quartered	15-ounce can black beans, rinsed and drained	1 tablespoon ground cumin
		$1/2$ teaspoon sea salt

1. Heat the oil in a large skillet over medium-low heat. Add the scallions, garlic, bell pepper, and celery, and sauté for 3 minutes or until beginning to soften. Remove from the heat and set aside.

2. Place the black beans in a blender or food processor, and pulse to form a chunky purée. Add the sautéed vegetables and continue to pulse about 10 seconds or until well distributed. (Do not clean the skillet, as it will be used to cook the sliders.)

3. Transfer the mixture to a large bowl. Add the oat flour, cilantro, cumin, and sea salt, and stir until well combined.

4. Form the mixture into 2-inch rounds about $1/2$ inch thick.

5. Heat up the skillet over medium heat. Add the sliders and cook about 4 minutes on each side until browned. Serve as is or with your favorite toppings.

Black Bean and Quinoa Burgers

Yield: 4 burgers

1/2 cup quinoa, rinsed and drained

3/4 cup water

6 scallions, sliced

1 celery stalk, sliced

3 cloves garlic, quartered

15-ounce can black beans, rinsed and drained

1 tablespoon ground cumin

1/2 teaspoon sea salt

1/4 teaspoon black pepper

1/4 teaspoon curry powder

1–2 tablespoons extra-virgin olive oil

Enjoy these hearty burgers plain or topped with your favorite condiment. Try a dollop of Mummy's Yummy Hummus (page 50), a spoonful of Chunky Corn Relish (page 43), or some Super Salsa (page 42).

1. Bring the quinoa and water to boil in a small pot over high heat. Reduce the heat to low, cover, and simmer for 12 to 14 minutes, or until the water is absorbed and the quinoa is tender. Remove from the heat, and set aside.

2. Add the scallions, celery, and garlic to a food processor, and pulse to coarsely chop. Add the cooked quinoa and all of the remaining ingredients. Pulse until the mixture is well combined but slightly chunky.

3. Form handfuls of the mixture into 4-inch round patties about 1/2 inch thick.

4. Heat the oil in a large skillet over medium heat. Add the patties and cook about 4 minutes on each side until browned.

5. Serve as is or in gluten-free buns.

CHANGE IT UP . . .

- For a "meatier" taste, add 1 cup sautéed mushroom slices.
- For a bit of crunch, add 3/4 cup toasted sunflower seeds.

Hearty Corn and Black Bean Tacos

These tasty tacos are loaded with a hearty filling of sweet corn and savory black beans.

1. Place the beans, salsa, garlic, and cumin in a medium pot, and simmer over medium heat for 5 to 8 minutes.

2. While the beans are simmering, heat the oil in a medium skillet over medium-low heat. Add the corn, black pepper, and cayenne pepper, and cook about 5 minutes while stirring frequently. Add the onion and cilantro, reduce the heat to low, and cook another 2 to 3 minutes or until the onion begins to soften.

3. Add the corn mixture to the bean mixture, reduce the heat to medium-low, and simmer about 5 minutes or until heated through. Remove from the heat and set aside.

4. Stack the tortillas, wrap them in foil, and warm in a 350°F oven or toaster oven for 5 to 7 minutes.

5. Spoon the filling into each warm tortilla, top with lettuce, and serve.

CHANGE IT UP . . .

- For added heat, increase the amount of cayenne pepper and/or add a finely chopped jalapeño chile to the filling.

Yield: 4 tacos

1 cup cooked black beans

$1/2$ cup Super Salsa (page 42), or commercial variety

2 cloves garlic, minced

2 teaspoons ground cumin

2 tablespoons extra-virgin olive oil

1 cup cooked corn kernels

$1/4$ teaspoon black pepper

$1/8$ teaspoon cayenne pepper

1 small red onion, diced

$1/4$ cup chopped fresh cilantro

4 corn tortillas (6-inch rounds)

Chopped romaine lettuce for garnish

Polenta Casserole

*This Mexican-inspired cornmeal casserole
is always a delectable hit!*

Yield: 10 to 12 servings

2 tablespoons extra-virgin olive oil

1 small onion, finely chopped

1 medium red bell pepper, finely chopped

4 cloves garlic, minced

15-ounce can black beans, rinsed and drained

$1^1/_2$ cups diced tomatoes

1 tablespoons chili powder, or to taste

1 tablespoon ground cumin

$^1/_4$ teaspoon cayenne pepper

2 tubes (16 ounces each) cooked polenta

2 cups soy-free vegan cheddar cheese shreds

1 cup Super Salsa (page 42), or commercial variety

$^1/_4$ cup chopped fresh cilantro

1. Preheat the oven to 375°F. Lightly oil a 3-quart rectangular baking dish and set aside.

2. Heat the oil in a medium skillet over medium-low heat. Add the onion, bell pepper, and garlic, and sauté 3 to 5 minutes or until beginning to soften.

3. Add the beans, tomatoes, chili powder, cumin, and cayenne pepper to the skillet. Stirring often, cook for about 10 minutes.

4. While the bean mixture is cooking, cut one tube of polenta into $1/_2$-inch cubes. Place the cubes in the bottom of the prepared baking dish, and press into an even layer.

5. Sprinkle 1 cup of the cheese over the polenta. Top with the bean mixture and half the salsa.

6. Cut the remaining tube of polenta into $1/2$-inch rounds and arrange over the bean mixture. Top with the remaining salsa and sprinkle with the remaining cheese.

7. Bake for 30 to 35 minutes or until the polenta is golden brown and the casserole is hot and bubbling. Remove from the oven, sprinkle with cilantro, and let stand about 10 minutes. Cut into squares and serve.

Quinoa Pasta 'n Veggies

Quinoa pasta is tossed with a delicious blend
of sautéed vegetables in this savory dish.

Yield: 2 servings

8 ounces elbow-shaped quinoa pasta

2 tablespoons extra-virgin olive oil

1 medium red onion, thinly sliced

2 cups sliced mushrooms

$1 1/2$ cups fresh asparagus ($1/2$-inch pieces)

1 cup fresh or frozen peas

1 tablespoon chopped fresh basil, or 1 teaspoon dried

1 teaspoon sea salt

1. Cook the pasta al dente according to package directions. Do not overcook. Drain the pasta and return to the pot.

2. While the pasta is cooking, heat the oil in a large skillet over medium-low heat. Add the onion and garlic, and sauté 3 to 5 minutes or until beginning to soften. Add the mushrooms, asparagus, and peas, and continue to sauté for 5 to 8 minutes or until the vegetables are tender.

3. Add the sautéed vegetables to the pasta, along with the basil and salt. Toss well. Serve immediately as is or with a sprinkling of vegan Parmesan.

Italian Noodle Casserole

This casserole is reminiscent of classic Italian lasagna.

Yield: 4 servings

2 cups elbow-shaped rice or quinoa pasta

2 tablespoons extra-virgin olive oil

1 cup sliced mushrooms

2 medium stalks celery, diced

1 medium yellow onion, finely chopped

3 cloves garlic, minced

1 cup tomato sauce

2 tablespoons chopped fresh basil, or 2 teaspoons dried

2 cups shredded soy-free vegan mozzarella cheese

1. Preheat the oven to 350°F. Lightly oil an 8-inch square casserole dish and set aside.

2. Cook the pasta al dente according to package directions. Drain, rinse under cold water, and drain again. Place in a large mixing bowl.

3. Heat the oil in a medium skillet over medium-low heat. Add the mushrooms, celery, onion, and garlic, and sauté 2 to 3 minutes or until beginning to soften.

4. Add the tomato sauce, basil, and 1³⁄₄ cups of the mozzarella to the pasta, and stir. Add the sautéed vegetables and continue to stir.

5. Spoon the mixture into the prepared casserole dish. Sprinkle with the remaining cheese, and cook 20 to 25 minutes or until the cheese is melted and the casserole is hot and bubbling.

Hearty Vegetable Stew

*This savory stew is delicious plain or topped with a sprinkling
of soy-free vegan cheddar or mozzarella. We find it
even better the next day.*

Yield: 6 servings

2 tablespoons extra-virgin olive oil

1 large yellow onion, quartered

3 cloves garlic, minced

3 large carrots, thickly sliced

3 celery stalks, thickly sliced

2¹/₂ cups thickly sliced mushrooms

¹/₂ cup mushroom or vegetable stock

4 medium tomatoes, diced

3 medium red potatoes, cut into 1-inch chunks

15-ounce can kidney beans

15-ounce can tomato sauce

1 bay leaf

1 tablespoon chopped fresh basil, or 1 teaspoon dried

1 tablespoon chopped fresh thyme, or 1 teaspoon dried

1 teaspoon sea salt

¹/₄ teaspoon curry powder

3 tablespoons oat flour

1. Heat the oil in a large pot over medium-low heat. Add the onion, garlic, carrots, celery, and mushrooms. Sauté for 4 to 5 minutes or until beginning to soften.

2. Add the stock and all of the remaining ingredients except the flour to the pot. Increase the heat and bring to a boil. Reduce the heat to low, cover, and simmer 25 to 30 minutes or until the vegetables are tender.

3. Place about 1 cup of the broth into a small bowl, add the oat flour, and stir until well combined. Return to the pot and cook another 5 minutes while stirring frequently.

4. Remove the bay leaf. Ladle the hot stew into bowls and serve.

EVERYBODY LOVES PIZZA!

Most people enjoy pizza, and for obvious reasons. It's delicious, fun to eat, and lends itself to lots of flavorful toppings. The good news is that everyone—even those with food allergies—can enjoy pizza.

The foundation of any pizza is the crust. With the growing number of commercial bread products that are. gluten- and allergen-free, items like pita rounds and bagels, as well as corn or rice tortillas can make great pizza crusts. A number of manufacturers like Bob's Red Mill and Authentic Foods carry pizza crust mixes that are gluten-free, dairy-free, and can be made without eggs. If you want to try your hand at making your own crust from scratch, be sure to check out our Perfect Pizza Crust (page 138). Also be aware that there are many decent crust recipes on the Internet.

A layer of rich tomato-based sauce traditionally covers the crust. Although there are many commercial sauces you can choose, our Quick 'n Easy Pizza Sauce (page 140)—it's a family recipe created by our Grandmother Giovanna, who came from a province in Tuscany. Of course, you can skip the tomato sauce altogether and use basil pesto (nut free) or even a simple brushing of olive oil.

Another classic pizza ingredient is cheese—specifically mozzarella and Parmesan varieties. For those with a dairy allergy, cheese has always been the most difficult ingredient to replace. A number of dairy-free cheeses are on the market, but finding one that is similar to dairy varieties has been challenging. We recommend Daiya brand vegan mozzarella, which we have found to be pretty close in taste, texture, and melting capabilities to the dairy variety (it's deliciously stretchy and gooey). And although we have yet to find a perfect substitute for Parmesan cheese, a number of decent vegan varieties are available. We have also found that a sprinkling of nutritional yeast flakes offers a rich, slightly cheesy flavor that resembles the taste of Parmesan.

When it comes to toppings, there is no shortage of ingredients thanks to the wide variety of fresh vegetables, legumes, herbs, and spices that are available. Here are some of our favorites:

- Artichoke hearts
- Asparagus tips
- Avocados
- Basil
- Bell peppers (all colors)
- Black beans

- Broccoli florets
- Capers
- Cherry tomatoes
- Chickpeas
- Eggplant
- Fennel

- Garlic
- Kale
- Mushrooms
- Olives
- Onions
- Oregano

- Rosemary
- Scallions
- Spinach
- Sun-dried tomatoes
- Tomatoes
- Zucchini

Over the years we have created some really sensational allergen-free pizzas with delicious ingredient combinations—some simple, others more complex. One thing we have learned is that when it comes to toppings, less is usually better. Too many flavors tend to compete with one another, so we try to limit toppings (not including herbs and spices) to two or three.

❑ Pesto with sliced tomatoes.

❑ Sautéed sliced mushrooms and caramelized onions.

❑ Sliced tomato, chopped red onion, and fresh basil.

❑ Sun-dried tomatoes, marinated artichoke hearts, and black olives.

❑ Black beans, diced tomatoes, and chopped scallions.

❑ Grilled eggplant, yellow bell pepper, and sliced red onion.

❑ Thinly sliced potatoes, chopped onions, and rosemary.

Below, we have shared a few of our favorites with you. Hope you enjoy trying them out, as well as creating specialty pizzas of your own.

Top any of the following combinations with vegan mozzarella, Parmesan, cheddar, and/or a sprinkling of nutritional yeast flakes. Also season as desired with herbs and spices, including salt and pepper.

❑ Grilled zucchini slices, sliced onions, and sautéed mushrooms.

❑ Broccoli florets, roasted bell pepper, and roasted garlic.

❑ Salsa, corn kernels, kidney beans, and fresh cilantro.

❑ Avocado, sun-dried tomatoes, and olives.

❑ Steamed asparagus tips, roasted red bell pepper, and fresh basil.

❑ Artichoke hearts, capers, and garlic.

❑ Sautéed kale, halved cherry tomatoes, and chopped scallions.

❑ Herb combo (basil, oregano, and rosemary), black olives, and olive oil.

FAVORITE NO-BAKE PIZZAS

❑ Spread a thick layer of Mummy's Yummy Hummus (page 50) on a lightly toasted corn tortilla. Top with chopped tomatoes, chopped scallions, corn kernels, and fresh cilantro.

❑ Toss shredded lettuce, grated carrots, halved cherry tomatoes, and sliced black olives with a vinaigrette dressing. Place over a prebaked pizza crust for a "salad pizza."

Perfect Pizza Crust

Mama Mia!
This allergen-free/gluten-free dough
makes a great pizza crust.

Yield: 4 thin crusts (8-inch rounds)

2¼ teaspoons active dry yeast (¼-ounce packet)

1½ cups warm (not hot) water

1 teaspoon honey

2 tablespoons olive oil

1½ teaspoons dried Italian seasoning blend

1 teaspoon sea salt

2 cups brown rice flour

1½ cups tapioca flour

1. Dissolve the yeast in a cup or small bowl with ½ cup of the warm water and the honey. The mixture should bubble up and foam within a minute or so. If it doesn't, the yeast is not good. Discard it and start over with fresh yeast.

2. Transfer the dissolved yeast to a large mixing bowl along with the remaining warm water, the oil, Italian seasoning blend, and salt. Stir well with a wooden spoon.

3. Add 1 cup of the brown rice flour to the bowl and stir well. Continue to stir while adding the remaining brown rice flour and tapioca flour. When the dough becomes too stiff to stir and starts pulling away from the sides of the bowl, it's time to knead.

4. Turn the dough (it will be sticky) onto a clean surface that has been sprinkled with rice flour. Knead the dough for 4 or 5 minutes, while continuing to sprinkle with flour, until it is smooth and no longer sticky.

5. Place the dough in a large, well-oiled bowl, then turn it over so the top is coated with oil. Coating the dough will keep it from

drying out. (You can use the same bowl you used to mix the ingredients, and you don't have to clean it first.) Cover the bowl with a clean damp dishtowel or plastic wrap. Place in a warm spot for about 30 minutes or until the dough doubles in bulk.

6. Preheat the oven to 400°F. Lightly oil a baking sheet and set aside.

7. Punch down the risen dough, fold it over a few times, then let rest a minute.

8. Divide the dough into 4 equal pieces and shape into balls.

9. Place each ball between sheets of waxed paper and roll out to 10-inch circles about $1/8$ inch thick. Pinch the edges with your fingers to create a slightly raised border.

10. Place the rounds on the prepared baking sheet and bake for 8 to 10 minutes. Remove from the oven, add the desired toppings, then return to the oven for an additional 15 to 20 minutes or until the bottom of the crust is browned.

CHANGE IT UP . . .

- For added crunch, sprinkle the oiled baking sheet with a handful of cornmeal before adding the dough. The cornmeal will bake into the bottom of the crusts, just like those made in a pizzeria!

- For dough that is a bit flaky and doesn't rise as much, use oat flour instead of the brown rice/tapioca flour combo.

- For more great pizza crust ideas, see "Everybody Loves Pizza!" on page 136.

AND BE AWARE THAT . . .

You can also prebake the crusts for 15 to 20 minutes, freeze them, and finish baking (with toppings) at a later time. Just be sure to cool the crusts completely. Wrap them individually in plastic wrap, place in a freezer-quality storage bag, and then freeze up to two months.

Quick 'n Easy Pizza Sauce

When fresh tomatoes and herbs weren't available, our Grandma Giovanna made this quick and easy tomato sauce. Perfect for pizza as well as pasta.

Yield: About 4 cups

3 tablespoons extra-virgin olive oil

1 medium yellow onion, diced

1 clove garlic, minced

29-ounce can tomato purée

28-ounce can crushed tomatoes

1 tablespoon honey

1 tablespoon dried Italian herb seasoning

3 tablespoons chopped fresh basil, or 1 tablespoon dried

1/2 teaspoon sea salt

1. Heat the oil in a large pot over medium-low heat. Add the onion and garlic, and sauté 5 to 8 minutes or until the onion begins to soften.

2. Add all of the remaining ingredients and stir well.

3. Increase the heat to medium-high and bring the sauce to a boil. Reduce the heat to low and simmer uncovered, stirring often, for at least 30 minutes or until the sauce reaches the desired consistency. (The longer it simmers, the thicker it will become and the less acidic it will taste.).

4. Use immediately or refrigerate in an airtight container up to one week. Freeze up to six months.

Italian-style Spaghetti Squash

Spaghetti squash is nature's tasty gluten-free "pasta."

Yield: 2 servings

- 1 medium spaghetti squash
- 2 tablespoons extra-virgin olive oil
- 1 small yellow onion, finely chopped
- 2 cloves garlic, minced
- 1 cup sliced white button or crimini mushrooms
- 15-ounce can Italian-style diced tomatoes
- 1 tablespoon chopped fresh basil
- 1 teaspoon dried oregano
- $1/2$ teaspoon sea salt, or to taste

1. Preheat the oven to 400°F.

2. Cut the squash in half, poke holes in the skin with a fork, and scoop out the seeds. Place the halves cut side up in a baking dish. Add $1/4$-inch water to the dish, cover, and bake for 35 to 40 minutes or until the flesh is soft when pierced with a fork.

3. While the squash is baking, heat the oil in a large skillet over medium-low heat. Add the onion and garlic, and sauté 3 to 5 minutes or until beginning to soften.

4. Add the mushrooms to the skillet, sauté 2 to 3 minutes, then add the tomatoes and basil. Increase the heat to high and bring to a boil. Reduce the heat to low, cover and simmer at least 15 minutes. (The longer this sauce simmers, the better the flavor.)

5. Remove the cooked squash from the oven and let cool a bit. Using a fork, remove the spaghetti-like strands from the skin and transfer to a bowl. Add the sauce and toss well.

6. Serve as is or topped with a sprinkling of soy-free vegan Parmesan.

Neapolitan Baked Eggplant

These baked eggplant halves are really satisfying. We usually serve them alongside a fresh green salad and side of brown rice or quinoa—like the Quinoa Confetti on page 124.

Yield: 4 servings

2 medium eggplants

2 medium tomatoes, diced

1 teaspoon dried oregano

1/2 teaspoon black pepper

2 slices rice bread

4 cloves garlic, minced

1/2 cup pitted black olives

1/2 cup chopped fresh parsley

2 tablespoons rice milk

2 tablespoons extra-virgin olive oil

1 tablespoon capers

1. Preheat the oven to 350°F. Halve the eggplants lengthwise and place cut-side up in a lightly oiled baking dish. Set aside.

2. Place the tomatoes, oregano, and pepper in a mixing bowl. Toss well and set aside.

3. Tear up the bread and place in a blender or food processor along with remaining ingredients. Blend to a fairly smooth paste.

4. Spread the paste on each eggplant half, then top with the diced tomatoes.

5. Bake the eggplant for about 1 hour or until the flesh is soft and tender when pierced with a fork. Serve hot.

Easy
Pasta Primavera

*Fresh vegetables and flavorful herbs are tossed
with rice pasta in this tasty, satisfying dish.*

Yield: 4 servings

16 ounces rice pasta

1/4 cup extra-virgin
   olive oil

6 cloves garlic, minced

2 large carrots, cut into
   1/4-inch slices

4 scallions, chopped

10 thin asparagus spears,
   cut into 1/2-inch pieces

1 medium red bell pepper,
   diced

1 tablespoon dried Italian
   herb blend

2 teaspoons garlic powder

2 teaspoons sea salt

1 teaspoon black pepper

1/2 cup chopped fresh basil

1 large tomato, chopped

1. Cook the pasta according to package directions.

2. While the pasta is cooking, heat the oil in a large skillet over
   medium-low heat. Add the garlic, carrots, scallions, asparagus,
   and bell pepper, and sauté 5 to 7 minutes or until the vegetables
   are tender-crisp.

3. Sprinkle the vegetables with Italian herb blend, garlic powder,
   salt, and pepper. Sauté another minute.

4. Drain the cooked pasta and place in a large bowl. Add the
   sautéed vegetables, basil, and chopped tomato. Toss well.

5. Serve piping hot as is or with a sprinkling of soy-free vegan
   Parmesan cheese.

Veggie Lo Mein

We love this classic Asian-inspired dish,
which is loaded with both vegetables and flavor.

Yield: 2 servings

8 ounces gluten-free spaghetti

$3/4$ cup vegetable broth

2 tablespoons soy-free soy sauce or coconut aminos

1 tablespoon agave nectar

1 tablespoon arrowroot

$1/2$ teaspoon red pepper flakes

2 tablespoons extra-virgin olive oil

$1/2$ cup trimmed snow peas or snap peas

$1/2$ cup thinly sliced red bell pepper

1 cup mung bean sprouts

6 scallions, chopped

4 cloves garlic, minced

1 tablespoon minced fresh ginger

2 tablespoons toasted sesame seeds or hemp seeds (optional)

1. Cook the pasta according to package directions. Drain, rinse under cold water, and set aside.

2. Place the broth, soy-free soy sauce, agave nectar, arrowroot, and pepper flakes in a medium bowl. Stir well and set aside.

3. Heat the olive oil in a large skillet over medium-low heat. Add the snow peas, bell pepper, mung sprouts, and scallions, and sauté 4 to 5 minutes or until beginning to soften. Add the garlic and ginger, and continue to sauté another 2 minutes or until the vegetables are tender-crisp.

4. Add the broth mixture to the skillet, and simmer the ingredients while stirring for 3 to 4 minutes or until heated through. Add the pasta and toss well.

5. Transfer to a serving bowl, sprinkle with toasted sesame seeds (if using), and enjoy immediately.

ABOUT SUSHI ROLLS

When many people hear the word "sushi," they think of raw fish. Sushi actually refers to a number of Japanese dishes that are made with short-grain sticky rice that is flavored with sweetened vinegar. One of these dishes, which has become popular in the United States, is *nori-maki*—the sushi roll. These rolls contain rice and other ingredients that are rolled up in a sheet of toasted nori. (Nori is made from seaweed and rich in vitamins and minerals.) The roll is then cut into small bite-sized rounds that are often served with a dab of pungent wasabi paste and slices of pickled ginger.

For those who are allergic to one or more of the major allergenic foods, the sushi roll is a wonderful dietary choice. Along with rice, the filling can include a wide range of vegetable choices, which add both flavor and texture to these miniature bites. In addition to wasabi and pickled ginger, another traditional accompaniment for sushi rolls is soy sauce. If soy is an allergenic concern, coconut aminos make an excellent "soy sauce-like" substitute. (For more information, see "Coconut Aminos" below.)

Sushi rolls are also fairly easy to make. All it takes is a little practice and being aware of a few helpful guidelines. First, it is important that the rice is cooled to room temperature. Freshly made hot rice won't hold together well and the roll will fall apart. If the rice has been refrigerated, it must come to room temp first. To form the rolls, you will need a bamboo sushi mat, although a clean woven placement also works. Sushi mats are inexpensive and available in natural foods stores, Japanese markets, and many supermarkets. Finally, don't overpack the rolls. Cramming them with too much filling will prevent them from rolling up properly. It will also result in rounds that are too big and too hard to eat with one or two bites.

Making your own sushi rolls means there is no chance of cross-contamination from fish or shellfish—as there may be from sushi that is prepared in restaurants or sold in supermarkets. Be sure to try the Very Veggie Sushi Rolls on page 146. It is a basic recipe that offers clear step-by-step instructions and illustrations for forming the rolls. Enjoy!

COCONUT AMINOS
AN EXCEPTIONAL SOY SAUCE SUBSTITUTE

Rich, dark, and salty, coconut aminos is a delicious gluten- and soy-free soy sauce substitute that is very close in taste to the authentic product. Rich in amino acids, it is a simple, naturally aged blend of sea salt and raw sap from the coconut tree. Use it as you would soy sauce—in marinades, sauces, and salad dressings, and, of course, as a dipping sauce for sushi rolls. Be sure to try it with the Very Veggie Sushi Rolls on page 146.

Very Veggie Sushi Rolls

These delectable rice and vegetable bites make a great light lunch or dinner entrée, as well as an appetizing snack. The helpful illustrations at right will help guide you in their preparation. Also check out the tips presented in "About Sushi Rolls" on page 145.

Yield: 6 sushi rolls
(48 bite-sized rounds)

• • • • • • • • • •

3 cups short-grain
brown rice, rinsed
and drained

6 cups water

2/3 cup rice wine vinegar

3 tablespoons agave nectar

2 small carrots, cut into
julienne strips

1 small zucchini, cut
into julienne strips

1 small cucumber, seeded
and cut into julienne strips

6 sheets toasted nori

OPTIONAL ACCOMPANIMENTS

Wasabi paste

Pickled ginger

Coconut aminos*

* Soy sauce alternative (see page 145).

1. Bring the rice and water to boil in a medium pot. Reduce the heat to low, stir once, and cover. Cook 45 to 50 minutes or until the liquid is absorbed and the rice is tender.

2. While the rice is cooking, blanch the carrots in boiling water for 1 to 2 minutes or until tender-crisp. Drain and set aside. Stir the vinegar and agave nectar together until well blended. Set aside.

3. Transfer the cooked rice to a large bowl. Pour the vinegar-agave mixture over the rice, then gently mix (this is best done with a wide, flat spatula or wooden spoon). Don't stir or mix the rice, as it will become mushy and clump up. Let cool to room temperature.

4. To prepare the rolls, place a sheet of nori (shiny side down) on the sushi mat. Spread a handful or two of the cooled rice on top of the nori, leaving a 2-inch border on the top and bottom (the two longer sides). With slightly moist hands, flatten the rice gently but firmly into an even layer.

5. Place a row of the julienned carrots, cucumbers, and zucchini lengthwise across the center of the rice (see Step 1 at right).

6. Lightly moisten the top border of nori with water. Then, beginning at the bottom, carefully roll up the nori using the sushi mat (see Step 2 at right). While rolling, apply firm but gentle pressure. The moistened edge of the nori will seal the roll.

7. Continue making rolls with the remaining nori and filling. If you are not serving them right away, wrap the rolls in plastic wrap and refrigerate.

8. To serve, slice each roll into 8 rounds (see Step 3 at right). Serve as is or with wasabi, pickled ginger, and/or coconut aminos.

CHANGE IT UP . . .

• Spread a line of wasabi on the rice along with the other filling ingredients.

• Try other vegetables for the filling. Here are just a few recommendations:

    asparagus spears, blanched

    avocado

    beets, roasted

    bell peppers, roasted

    daikon radish, fresh or pickled

    jicama

    kale, shredded

    mushrooms, sautéed and chopped

    scallions

    sweet potatoes, cooked

1. Spread the rice on a sheet of nori. Add a row of julienned carrots, cucumbers, and zucchini across the center.

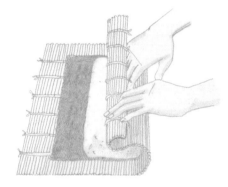

2. Roll up the filled nori with the sushi mat.

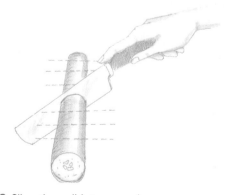

3. Slice the roll into rounds.

Gingery Mint Spirals

*Brown rice pasta is tossed in a lemony garlic sauce
with added flavors of fresh mint and ginger.*

Yield: 4 servings

1 pound brown rice
spiral pasta

1/2 cup lemon juice

1/4 cup extra-virgin
olive oil

1/4 cup chopped scallions

1/4 cup chopped fresh
mint leaves

1 tablespoon diced fresh
ginger, or 1 teaspoon dried

1 teaspoon sea salt

1. Cook the pasta al dente according to package directions.
   Do not overcook. Drain the pasta and return to the pot.

2. While the pasta is cooking, place the remaining ingredients
   in blender or food processor, and blend to a smooth sauce.

3. Pour the sauce over the pasta, stir well, and heat up over
   low heat. Serve immediately.

CHANGE IT UP . . .

- Instead of brown rice pasta, try using quinoa pasta or
  soba noodles.

Mac 'n Cheese

This classic dish is a kid-pleasing favorite (for kids of all ages).

Yield: 2 servings

8 ounces elbow-shaped
quinoa pasta or rice pasta

2 tablespoons vegan
margarine

1 cup rice milk

2 cups soy-free vegan
cheddar cheese shreds

1 tablespoon nutritional
yeast

1/8 teaspoon black pepper

Dash paprika (optional)

1. Cook the pasta al dente according to package directions. Do
   not overcook. Drain the pasta and return to the pot.

2. Melt the margarine in a medium pot over medium-low heat.
   Add the rice milk, cheddar shreds, nutritional yeast, and
   pepper, and stir to form a smooth sauce.

3. Pour the sauce over the pasta, stir well, and heat up over
   low heat.

4. Serve hot with a sprinkling of paprika. Store leftovers (if there
   are any) in the refrigerator up to five days.

9

Desserts and Treats

When it comes to cookies, muffins, and other sweet treats, the word "healthy" doesn't usually come to mind. That's because they are generally highly processed commercial products that are made with refined flour, artificial flavorings and colorings, hydrogenated oil, and preservatives. Their sweetness typically comes from refined sugar, high-fructose corn syrup, or artificial sweeteners. The healthier alternatives in this chapter are sweetened with agave nectar, brown rice syrup, honey, pure maple syrup, and fresh and dried fruit. They are also made with allergen-free/gluten-free flours and other ingredients, making them safe choices for those with food allergies. But most important—they are absolutely delicious.

In this chapter, we've shared an outstanding variety of our favorite desserts and sweet treats. They are recipes we have made many times for our families—and each one has gotten a two-thumbs-up approval rating (especially from our kids).

Among our cookie recipes, you will find classic choices like our oatmeal raisin cookies, which never fail to please. Our light and chewy Lemon Drops are bursting with flavor, while the ever-popular Mrs. Marple's Maple Meltaways have a rich "peanut-buttery" taste—only without the peanuts! When it comes to no-bake varieties, you'll find that our Carob-Coconut Balls and the No-Bake Maple Treats are rich, delicious, and a snap to make.

Our muffins, which include such favorites as Classic Blueberry, Carrot Cake, and Best Banana, are all made in standard-size muffin tins. You can, however, use the batter to make jumbo or mini varieties instead. A recipe that yields twelve standard (2 ¾ inch) muffins, makes six jumbo (3 inch) or thirty-two mini (1 ½ inch) muffins.

Other sweet treats in this chapter include such popular choices as Carob Fudge Brownies, Crispy Rice Treats, Acai Sorbet, Tropical Cobbler, Luscious Lemon Squares, Grilled Peaches à la Mode, and much more. All are healthful and easy to prepare. Best of all, they taste great and will satisfy even your strongest dessert cravings. Enjoy!

Carrot Cake Muffins

*Pineapple and raisins give this delectable
muffin classic carrot-cake flavor!*

Yield: 12 muffins

. . . .

2 cups Gluten-Free Baking Mix
(page 151), or commercial
variety

1 1/2 teaspoons baking powder

2 teaspoons ground cinnamon

1/4 teaspoon ground nutmeg

2 cups grated carrot

3/4 cup raisins

1/2 cup crushed pineapple

2/3 cup honey, agave nectar,
or pure maple syrup

2/3 cup water

1/2 cup safflower, sunflower,
coconut, or grapeseed oil

1. Preheat the oven to 350°F.

2. Combine the baking mix, baking powder, cinnamon, and nutmeg in a large bowl. Add the carrots, raisins, and pineapple, and stir until well distributed.

3. Blend together the honey, water, and oil. Add to the dry mixture, and stir to form a thick batter.

4. Spoon about 2 heaping tablespoons of batter into the cups of a greased or paper-lined standard muffin tin.

5. Bake for 20 to 25 minutes or until a toothpick inserted into the center of a muffin comes out clean.

6. Cool the muffins at least 10 minutes before removing from the tin.

ABOUT GLUTEN-FREE FLOURS AND BAKING MIXES

When it comes to gluten-free baking, we have found that for many items, such as cookies and pie crusts, simple flours like oat flour or brown rice flour works well. Brown rice flour can, however, be a bit grainy. For this reason, for most baked goods, we recommend using extra-fine brown rice flour, which is available in most natural foods stores.

For many other baked goods like cakes and muffins, we have found a combination of flours works best. Gluten-free baking mixes, such as Bob's Red Mill Baking Mix and Trader Joe's Gluten-Free Baking Mix are good choices. If, however, you would like to create your own mix, try the following recipe on page 151. We always have some on hand to use at a moment's notice.

Gluten-Free Baking Mix

1. Combine all of the ingredients in a gallon-size zip-lock freezer bag. Shake until well blended.

2. Store in an airtight container in the refrigerator up to three months, or in the freezer up to six months.

Yield: About 6 cups

4 cups brown rice flour (preferably extra-fine)

1 1/2 cups potato starch

2/3 cup tapioca flour

4 teaspoons xanthan gum*

* This gluten-free ingredient acts as the "glue" that holds baked goods together and helps them rise (a characteristic function of gluten).

Classic Blueberry Muffins

These muffins are light, fluffy, and bursting with blueberries.

1. Preheat the oven to 350°F.

2. Combine the flour, baking powder, and cinnamon in a medium bowl. Add the blueberries and stir until well distributed.

3. Place the honey, rice milk, applesauce, oil, and vanilla in a large bowl and stir until well blended. Add the flour mixture and stir to form a thick batter.

4. Spoon about 2 heaping tablespoons of batter into the cups of a greased or paper-lined standard muffin tin.

5. Bake for 20 to 25 minutes or until a toothpick inserted into the center of a muffin comes out clean.

6. Cool the muffins at least 10 minutes before removing from the tin.

Yield: 12 muffins

2 cups brown rice flour (preferably extra-fine)

1 teaspoon baking powder

1 teaspoon ground cinnamon

3 cups fresh or frozen blueberries*

1 cup honey, agave nectar, or pure maple syrup

1/2 cup rice milk

1/2 cup applesauce

1/4 cup safflower, sunflower, coconut, or grapeseed oil

1 teaspoon vanilla

* If using frozen blueberries, defrost and pat dry.

Apple-Blueberry Muffins

The combination of apples and blueberries
add natural sweetness to these heavenly muffins.

Yield: 12 muffins

2 cups Gluten-Free Baking
Mix (page 151), or
commercial variety

1 tablespoon baking
powder

1 teaspoon ground
cinnamon

1 cup diced apples
(preferably Granny Smith
or Pippin)

1 cup fresh or frozen
blueberries*

2/3 cup honey, agave nectar,
or pure maple syrup

2/3 cup water

1/2 cup applesauce

1 teaspoon vanilla

* If using frozen blueberries,
defrost and pat dry.

1. Preheat the oven to 350°F.

2. Combine the baking mix, baking powder, and cinnamon in a
   medium bowl. Add the apples and blueberries, and stir until well
   distributed.

3. Place the honey, water, applesauce, and vanilla in a large bowl
   and stir until well blended. Add the dry mixture and stir to form
   a thick batter.

4. Spoon about 2 heaping tablespoons of batter into the cups of
   a greased or paper-lined standard muffin tin.

5. Bake for 20 to 25 minutes or until a toothpick inserted into the
   center of a muffin comes out clean.

6. Cool the muffins at least 10 minutes before removing from the tin.

Best Banana Muffins

Whenever ripe bananas are on hand, keep this recipe in mind.
Your family will thank you every time.

Yield: 12 muffins

2 cups Gluten-Free Baking
   Mix (page 151), or
   commercial variety

1 teaspoon baking powder

1 teaspoon baking soda

1 teaspoon ground
   cinnamon

1 1/3 cups mashed ripe
   bananas

3/4 cup honey, agave nectar,
   or pure maple syrup

1/2 cup safflower, sunflower,
   coconut, or grapeseed oil

1 teaspoon vanilla

1. Preheat the oven to 350°F.

2. Combine the baking mix, baking powder, baking soda, and cinnamon in a medium bowl.

3. Place the bananas, honey, oil, and vanilla in a large bowl and stir until well blended. Add the dry mixture and stir to form a thick batter.

4. Spoon about 2 heaping tablespoons of batter into the cups of a greased or paper-lined standard muffin tin.

5. Bake for 18 to 20 minutes or until a toothpick inserted into the center of a muffin comes out clean.

6. Cool the muffins at least 10 minutes before removing from the tin.

CHANGE IT UP . . .

• For added sweetness and texture, add 1 cup of raisins to the mixture in Step 2, and stir until well distributed.

Simply Pumpkin Muffins

These delicately sweet muffins are always delicious,
but we find them best warm and fresh from the oven.
Sometimes, we top them with a scoop of dairy-free "ice cream."

Yield: 10 muffins

$^2/_3$ cup brown rice flour
(preferably extra-fine)

$^1/_2$ cup oat flour

$^1/_2$ cup arrowroot flour

1$^1/_2$ teaspoons baking
powder

2 teaspoons ground
cinnamon

$^1/_2$ teaspoon ground
nutmeg

$^1/_2$ cup raisins

1$^1/_2$ cups pumpkin purée

$^3/_4$ cup honey, agave
nectar, or pure
maple syrup

$^1/_2$ cup safflower,
sunflower, coconut,
or grapeseed oil

1. Preheat the oven to 350°F.

2. Combine the flours, baking powder, cinnamon, and nutmeg in
   a medium bowl. Add the raisins and stir until well distributed.

3. Place the pumpkin purée, honey, and oil in a large bowl and
   stir until well blended. Add the flour mixture and stir to form
   a thick batter.

4. Spoon about 2 heaping tablespoons of batter into the cups of
   a greased or paper-lined standard muffin tin.

5. Bake for 30 to 35 minutes or until a toothpick inserted into the
   center of a muffin comes out clean.

6. Cool the muffins at least 10 minutes before removing from the tin.

Lemon Drops

*If you like the fresh taste of lemon,
these light chewy cookies are for you.*

Yield: About 16 cookies

. . . .

1 tablespoon flaxseed meal

2 tablespoons warm water

1 cup brown rice flour (preferably extra-fine)

1 teaspoon baking powder

$\frac{1}{2}$ cup unsweetened flaked coconut

$\frac{1}{3}$ cup coconut sugar or date sugar

$\frac{1}{2}$ cup lemon juice

3 tablespoons safflower, sunflower, coconut, or grapeseed oil

1 teaspoon vanilla

1. Preheat the oven to 350°F. Lightly oil a cookie sheet or line with parchment paper. Set aside.

2. In a cup or small bowl, mix together the flaxseed meal and water, and let sit for a minute.

3. Combine the flour and baking powder in a medium bowl. Add the coconut and stir until well distributed. Set aside.

4. Place the coconut sugar, lemon juice, oil, vanilla, and flaxseed mixture in a large mixing bowl and stir until well blended.

5. Add the flour mixture to the lemon mixture and stir to form a thick batter-like dough.

6. Drop rounded tablespoons of dough about 2 inches apart on the prepared cookie sheet.

7. Bake for 10 to 12 minutes or until lightly browned.

8. Cool the cookies a few minutes before removing from the sheet. Transfer to a wire rack to finish cooling.

Classic Oatmeal Raisin Cookies

This cookie classic is one of our family favorites.
Everyone loves them!

Yield: About 30 cookies

1 1/2 cups oat flour

1 teaspoon baking powder

2 teaspoons ground cinnamon

3 cups rolled oats

1 cup raisins

1 cup honey

2/3 cup safflower, sunflower, coconut, or grapeseed oil

1 tablespoon vanilla

1. Preheat the oven to 350°F. Lightly oil a cookie sheet or line with parchment paper. Set aside.

2. Combine the flour, baking powder, and cinnamon in a medium bowl. Add the oats and raisins, and stir until well distributed. Set aside.

3. Place the honey, oil, and vanilla in a large mixing bowl and stir until well blended.

4. Add the flour mixture to the honey mixture and stir to form a sticky batter-like dough.

5. Drop rounded tablespoons of dough about 2 inches apart on the prepared cookie sheet.

6. Bake for 10 to 12 minutes or until lightly browned.

7. Cool the cookies a few minutes before removing from the sheet. Transfer to a wire rack to finish cooling. Serve warm or at room temperature.

CHANGE IT UP . . .

- For added flavor and texture, add 1 cup of toasted sunflower seeds or unsweetened shredded coconut to the batter.

- For a chewy, moister cookie, substitute the oil with an equal amount of applesauce.

- Olive oil's distinctive taste is generally not suitable for baked goods, but it works in this recipe. When using olive oil, reduce the honey to $3/4$ cup and add $1/3$ cup pure maple syrup for a sweeter taste—or omit the honey altogether and use 1 cup maple syrup.

Carob-Coconut Balls

These no-bake treats are simple to make and absolutely delicious.

1. Combine the coconut and carob in a medium bowl.

2. Place the oil, agave, and vanilla in a large mixing bowl, and stir until well blended.

3. Add the coconut mixture to the agave mixture and stir until well combined.

4. Form heaping tablespoons of the mixture into balls, and refrigerate at least 30 minutes.

5. Serve chilled. Store leftovers in a covered container up to one week.

Yield: About 14 balls

3 cups unsweetened shredded coconut

$1/2$ cup carob powder

$1/2$ cup coconut oil

$1/2$ cup agave nectar

1 tablespoon vanilla

CHANGE IT UP . . .

- For added sweetness and texture, stir $1/4$ cup raisins into the mixture in Step 3.

No-Bake Maple Treats

Yield: About 14 treats

I cup rolled oats

I cup Great Gluten-Free Granola (page 165), or commercial variety

$3/4$ cup toasted sunflower seeds

2 tablespoons toasted flaxseeds

I teaspoon ground cinnamon

$1/8$ teaspoon ground nutmeg

2 tablespoons applesauce

2 tablespoons pure maple syrup

Flaxseeds and sunflower seeds add wonderful crunch to these maple-rich cookies.

1. Spread out the oats on a baking sheet. Place in a preheated 350°F oven or toaster oven and bake for 10 to 15 minutes or until golden brown. Remove and let cool.

2. Place the cooled oats in a blender or food processor along with the granola, sunflower seeds, flaxseeds, cinnamon, and nutmeg. Pulse to a slightly coarse consistency.

3. Add the applesauce and maple syrup to the blender. Continue to pulse to form a moist dough.

4. Form heaping tablespoons of the dough into balls, and refrigerate at least 30 minutes.

5. Serve chilled. Store leftovers in a covered container up to one week.

Celery Boats

Yield: 4 to 5 servings

8 celery stalks, cut in half

$3/4$ cup sunflower seed butter

$1/2$ teaspoon ground cinnamon

Raisins for garnish

Kids especially love this easy-to-prepare snack.

1. Add the cinnamon to the sunflower seed butter, and stir well. Spoon or pipe the mixture into the celery halves.

2. Garnish with raisins before serving.

CHANGE IT UP . . .

- Fill the celery "boats" with Mummy's Yummy Hummus (page 50) instead of sunflower butter.

- If nuts are not an allergy concern, substitute almond, cashew, or other nut butter for the sunflower butter.

Grilled Peaches à la Mode

Peaches are among our favorite summer fruits. Grilling them adds delicious depth of flavor.

1. Combine all of the marinade ingredients in a large bowl. Add the peach halves and coat well. Marinate in the refrigerator about 4 hours.

2. Oil the grate of a heated grill. Arrange the peaches on top, and cook about 5 minutes on each side or until grill marks appear. Baste the peaches with marinade as they cook.

3. Serve warm topped with a scoop of nondairy ice cream.

Yield: 4 servings

2 peaches, halved

Vanilla nondairy ice cream

MARINADE

$1/3$ cup sunflower, safflower, or grapeseed oil

3 tablespoons coconut sugar

$1 1/2$ teaspoons ground cinnamon

Grated zest from 1 orange

5 cloves

1 tablespoon vanilla

$1/4$ teaspoon sea salt

Granny's Apple Crisp

For this recipe, green apple varieties like Granny Smith or Pippin, are the best (organic of course).

1. Preheat the oven to 350°F. Lightly oil a 9-inch square baking dish and set aside.

2. Combine all of the ingredients except the apples in a large bowl. Set aside.

3. Place the apples in the bottom of the prepared baking pan and cover with the oat mixture.

4. Bake for 50 to 55 minutes or until the topping is browned and crisp.

5. Serve warm or at room temperature.

Yield: 4 servings

$1/2$ cup rolled oats or quinoa flakes

$1/2$ cup oat flour

$1/2$ cup pure maple syrup

$1/3$ cup safflower, sunflower, coconut, or grapeseed oil

1 teaspoon ground cinnamon

1 teaspoon vanilla

4 cups diced Granny Smith apples, unpeeled

Mrs. Marple's Maple Meltaways

These delicate melt-in-your mouth cookies have a luscious "peanut buttery" taste without the peanuts.

Yield: About 20 cookies

2 cups oat flour

1 teaspoon baking powder

1 cup pure maple syrup

1 cup toasted sunflower seed butter

1/3 cup safflower, sunflower, coconut, or grapeseed oil

1 tablespoon vanilla

1. Preheat the oven to 350°F. Lightly oil a cookie sheet or line with parchment paper. Set aside.

2. Combine the flour and baking powder in a medium bowl and set aside.

3. Place the maple syrup, sunflower butter, oil, and vanilla in a large mixing bowl and stir until well blended.

4. Add the flour mixture to the maple mixture and stir to form a thick, sticky, batter-like dough.

5. Drop rounded tablespoons of dough about 2 inches apart on the prepared cookie sheet.

6. Bake for 10 to 12 minutes or until lightly browned.

7. Cool the cookies a few minutes before removing from the sheet. Transfer to a wire rack to finish cooling. Serve warm or at room temperature.

CHANGE IT UP . . .

- For added crunch, sprinkle the cookies with raw sunflower seeds before baking.

- Use sesame seed butter instead of sunflower.

- For added sweetness and texture, add 1/2 cup raisins to the batter.

- For a spark of citrus flavor, add 1/4 cup fresh lemon juice and some grated lemon zest in Step 3.

Carob
Fudge Brownies

We always make a double batch of these moist, delicious brownies—one to enjoy right away, and another to freeze and snack on later. We even like them while they're still frozen!

1. Preheat the oven to 350°F. Lightly oil a 13-x-9-inch baking pan and set aside.

2. Combine the flour, carob powder, and baking powder in a medium bowl. Set aside.

3. Place the honey, water, oil, and vanilla in a large mixing bowl and stir until well blended.

4. Add the flour mixture to the honey mixture and stir to form a smooth batter. Spoon the batter into the prepared pan and spread in an even layer.

5. Bake for 20 to 25 minutes or until a toothpick inserted into the middle of the brownie comes out clean. Remove the pan from the oven and place on a wire rack to cool.

6. Cool at least 10 minutes before cutting the brownie into squares and serving.

Yield: 12 brownies

2$^1/_2$ cups oat flour

$^3/_4$ cup carob powder

1 teaspoon baking powder

1$^3/_4$ cups honey or agave nectar

$^3/_4$ cup water

$^3/_4$ cup safflower, sunflower, coconut, or grapeseed oil

1 teaspoon vanilla

CHANGE IT UP . . .

- Instead of oat flour, try an equal amount of quinoa, rice, or teff flour.

- For added flavor and texture, add $^1/_3$ cup raisins or $^1/_2$ cup sunflower seeds to the batter.

- Instead of oil, you can use $^2/_3$ cup applesauce.

- For a sweet maple flavor, substitute 1$^1/_2$ cups pure maple syrup for the honey.

Crispy Rice Treats

Talk about the perfect no-bake snack! It's crunchy, flavorful, and lends itself to lots of variations.

Yield: 16 treats
. . . .

4 cups crispy brown rice cereal

1/2 cup toasted sunflower seeds

1/2 cup raisins

1 cup toasted sunflower seed butter

3/4 cup agave nectar, honey, or combination of both

1 teaspoon agar powder

1 teaspoon vanilla

1. Combine the brown rice cereal, sunflower seeds, and raisins in a large bowl and set aside.

2. Place the sunflower seed butter and agave nectar in a medium pot over medium-low heat. Heat while gently stirring for about 2 minutes or until smooth and creamy. Add the agar and vanilla, and continue to stir another minute. Remove from the heat and let cool a bit.

3. Pour the warm agave-sunflower mixture over the cereal mixture, and stir until well coated. Transfer to an unoiled 8-x-11-inch baking pan or glass baking dish.

4. With slightly wet hands, pat the mixture (it will be sticky) in an even layer—about $1^{1}/_{2}$ inches thick.

5. Refrigerate at least 1 hour or until firm. Cut into 2-inch squares and serve.

6. Refrigerate leftovers in an airtight container up to a week, or freeze up to two months.

CHANGE IT UP . . .

- Instead of (or in addition to) raisins, try other dried unsulfured fruit. Pineapple, mango, blueberries, cranberries, and apples are all recommended choices.

- Try adding pumpkin seeds, flaxseeds, sesame seeds, and/or unsweetened coconut to these treats.

- If nuts are not an allergy concern, substitute almond, cashew, or other nut butter for the sunflower seed butter.

Double-Energy Date Squares

These chewy squares make the perfect on-the-go snack.

Yield: 12 squares

• • • • • • • • •

1 cup pitted dates

4 cups oat flour

4 cups rolled oats

$3/4$ cup toasted sunflower seeds

1 tablespoon ground cinnamon

1 cup safflower, sunflower, coconut, or grapeseed oil

1 cup pure maple syrup

1 teaspoon vanilla

$1/2$ teaspoon sea salt

1. Cover the dates in hot water and let soak at least 1 hour or until soft.

2. Preheat the oven to 350°F. Lightly oil a 13-x-9-inch baking pan and set aside.

3. Drain the soaked dates and transfer to a blender or food processor. Blend to a thick purée.

4. Place the flour, oats, sunflower seeds, and cinnamon in a large bowl and mix well.

5. In another bowl, stir the oil, maple syrup, vanilla, and salt until well blended. Add to the flour mixture and mix well.

6. Transfer half the mixture to the prepared baking pan, and press into an even layer.

Spread the puréed dates on top, and cover with the remaining flour mixture.

7. Bake for 30 minutes or until lightly browned. Let cool before cutting into squares.

CHANGE IT UP . . .

• Try these squares warm with a scoop of sorbet on top.

• Instead of dates, use dried apricots or black mission figs.

Luscious Lemon Bars

Lemon bars—traditionally made with eggs and lots of white sugar—are dessert favorites. Here is an outstanding allergen-free version that is just as delicious.

Yield: 12 bars

. . . .

1 1/3 cups water

3 tablespoons agar flakes

2/3 cup fresh lemon juice

3 tablespoons arrowroot powder

3/4 cup coconut sugar

CRUST

2 cups rolled oats

1/2 cup coconut oil

2 tablespoons pure maple syrup

2 tablespoons water

1 tablespoon lemon juice

1 tablespoon vanilla

1. To prepare the crust, preheat the oven to 350°F. Lightly oil a 13-x-9-inch baking pan and set aside.

2. Place the oats in a blender or food processor and pulse to a slightly coarse, powdery mixture. Add the coconut oil and continue to pulse a few seconds until mixed. Add the remaining crust ingredients and pulse to form a doughy batter.

3. Add the batter to the prepared pan, and pat down in an even layer on the bottom and slightly up the sides. Bake for 12 to 15 minutes or until lightly browned. Remove and let cool.

4. To prepare the filling, place the water and agar in a medium pot, and let sit for 15 minutes.

5. In a small bowl, add the arrowroot to the lemon juice and stir to dissolve. Set aside.

6. Bring the agar mixture to a boil. Reduce the heat to low, and cook while stirring for 10 minutes or until the agar is completely dissolved. Stirring constantly, add the lemon juice-arrowroot mixture and coconut sugar. Continue to cook another 3 minutes or until the sugar has dissolved and the mixture has thickened (it will be tan in color).

7. Pour the filling into the prebaked crust and let sit about 20 minutes or until cooled.

8. Refrigerate at least 2 hours until chilled and well set. Cut into squares and serve.

Great Gluten-Free Granola

Along with enjoying this granola as a healthy snack, try it as a breakfast cereal topped with a splash of rice milk and some fresh fruit. Great way to start the day.

1. Preheat the oven to 350°F.

2. Place the oats, coconut, sunflower seeds, sesame seeds, raisins, and cinnamon in a large bowl and mix well. Set aside.

3. Heat the oil and honey in a small saucepan over medium heat for about a minute or until the mixture is well blended. Remove from the heat, add the vanilla, and stir well.

4. Pour the honey mixture over the oat mixture and stir until well coated.

5. Spread the mixture on an unoiled baking sheet and bake 7 or 8 minutes. Stir the mixture with a butter knife or spatula, then bake another 6 to 8 minutes or until browned and crisp.

6. Cool the granola completely before transferring to an airtight container or plastic zip-lock bag. Store in the pantry where it will keep up to a week. It will also keep in the freezer up to three months.

Yield: About 8 cups

5 cups rolled oats

2 cups unsweetened shredded coconut

1 cup raw sunflower seeds

$1/4$ cup raw sesame seeds

1 cup raisins

1 tablespoon ground cinnamon

$2/3$ cup safflower, sunflower, or coconut oil

$3/4$ cup honey, agave nectar, or pure maple syrup

1 tablespoon vanilla

CHANGE IT UP . . .

- For added flavor and texture, add a cup or so of puffed corn, puffed rice, or freeze-dried blueberries to the granola after it has cooled.

- If nuts are not an allergy concern, add some walnuts, cashews, or sliced almonds to the mix.

- Instead of rolled oats, use quinoa flakes or amaranth flakes.

Acai Sorbet

4 packages (4 ounces each) frozen acai pulp, thawed

$3/4$ cup agave nectar

2 tablespoons lemon juice

1 teaspoon vanilla

When agave nectar is added to slightly tart acai pulp, the flavor is similar to blueberries—and it makes a refreshing sorbet. Frozen acai pulp is available at most natural foods stores and many supermarkets.

1. Place all of the ingredients in a large bowl and stir or whisk until well blended. Pour into a sturdy 9-inch-square baking pan. (Do not use a disposable aluminum pan, which can easily puncture.)

2. Freeze for 30 to 40 minutes, then chop up the partially frozen mixture with a fork. Return to the freezer for another 30 to 40 minutes, chop again, and repeat another three or four times until the mixture is completely frozen.

3. Scoop the sorbet into bowls and serve. Freeze leftovers in a sealed airtight container up to one month.

MAKING FRUIT KABOBS
A FUN "SNACK-TIVITY" FOR KIDS

Just about everyone loves fruit, especially kids. And the fruit kabob is a great way for them to enjoy it. Threading a variety of bite-sized fruits on a skewer (we recommend bamboo sticks or wooden chopsticks) makes for a great kid-involved "snack-tivity"—one that is especially suitable for parties and play dates. And nothing can be easier or more fun for kids.

Just fill some bowls with a few different fruits (we've provided a list of our favorites below), hand them a skewer, and let them create their fresh 'n fruity masterpieces. As an added bonus, fruit kabobs freeze well.

- Apple wedges
- Honeydew chunks
- Pear wedges
- Banana chunks
- Kiwi slices
- Pineapple chunks
- Cantaloupe chunks
- Mango chunks
- Strawberries
- Grapes
- Orange sections
- Watermelon chunks

Creamy Raspberry-Orange Ice Pops

Easy-to-make and absolutely delicious.

1. Place all of the ingredients in a blender or food processor and blend until well combined.

2. Pour into six standard ice-pop molds, and freeze for 8 hours or overnight.

Yield: 6 ice pops

1 cup fresh or frozen raspberries

1 cup orange juice

1 cup coconut yogurt

2 tablespoons agave nectar

1 teaspoon vanilla

Fruity Ice Pops

These naturally sweet ice pops are made with chunks of real fruit. They are really refreshing, especially on hot summer days.

1. Purée the watermelon in a blender or food processor, and set aside.

2. Place an equal amount of bananas and blueberries in the bottom of six standard ice-pop molds.

3. Add watermelon purée to each mold, and freeze for 8 hours or overnight.

Yield: 6 ice pops

2 cups seedless watermelon chunks

2 ripe bananas, cut into chunks or slices

$1/2$ cup frozen blueberries

CHANGE IT UP . . .

• Lots of different fruits work for these pops. Raspberries, strawberries, and crushed pineapple are great choices.

Perfect Pumpkin Chewies

*Filled with spicy goodness, these chewy cookies
taste like pumpkin pie.*

Yield: About 40 cookies

2¹/₂ cups oat flour

I tablespoon baking powder

I tablespoon ground
cinnamon

I teaspoon ground nutmeg

I cup raisins

²/₃ cup rolled oats

I cup pumpkin purée

I cup pure maple syrup

¹/₂ cup safflower, sunflower,
coconut, or grapeseed oil

I teaspoon vanilla

1. Preheat the oven to 350°F. Lightly oil a cookie sheet or line with parchment paper. Set aside.

2. Combine the flour, baking powder, cinnamon, and nutmeg in a medium bowl. Add the raisins and oats, and stir until well distributed. Set aside.

3. Place the pumpkin purée, maple syrup, oil, and vanilla in a large mixing bowl and stir until well blended.

4. Add the flour mixture to the pumpkin mixture and stir until well combined.

5. Drop heaping tablespoons of the mixture about 2 inches apart on the prepared cookie sheet.

6. Bake for 10 to 12 minutes or until lightly browned.

7. Cool the cookies a few minutes before removing from the sheet. Transfer to a wire rack to finish cooling. Serve warm or at room temperature.

Pumpkin Custard Mini Cups

Here's a creamy, delicious no-bake filling that's great for pies, tarts, and our Mini Crunch Cups (page 60).

Yield: 12 mini cups

. . . .

3 tablespoons agar flakes

1/4 cup boiling water

1 cup rice milk

2/3 cup pure maple syrup

15-ounce can unsweetened pumpkin purée

1 teaspoon ground cinnamon

1/4 teaspoon ground ginger

1/4 teaspoon sea salt

1/8 teaspoon ground nutmeg

1 recipe Mini Crunch Cups (page 60)

1. Soak the agar flakes in the boiling water for 20 minutes.

2. Bring the rice milk, maple syrup, and soaked agar to boil in a medium pot. Reduce the heat to low, and simmer while stirring for about 3 minutes or until the agar is completely dissolved.

3. Add the pumpkin purée, cinnamon, ginger, salt, and nutmeg to the pot. Continue to stir and simmer for 1 minute or until the mixture is smooth and heated through. Remove from the heat and let cool.

4. Spoon the cooled filling mixture into the mini crunch cups, and refrigerate about 1 hour or until firm.

Cinnamon Tortilla Crisps

*These light, delicate cookie crisps go great
with a cold glass of rice milk or a cup of hot tea.*

Yield: 16 crisps

- 4 corn tortillas
  (6-inch rounds)
- 1/4 cup date sugar
- 2 teaspoons ground
  cinnamon
- 3 tablespoons safflower,
  sunflower, or grapeseed oil

1. Preheat the oven to 325°F.

2. Place the sugar and cinnamon in small bowl, stir to mix, and set aside.

3. Arrange the tortillas on a flat surface and lightly brush the tops with oil. Sprinkle with half the cinnamon-sugar mixture. Turn the tortillas over and lightly brush with oil. Cut each into quarters, then sprinkle with the remaining cinnamon-sugar.

4. Arrange the tortilla quarters on a large ungreased baking sheet. Bake for 8 minutes or until the tortillas begin to curl. Turn over and bake an additional 5 minutes or until brown and crisp. Be careful not to burn.

5. Allow the crisps to cool before serving.

Fresh Apricot Crisp

*Delicate-flavored apricots are spotlighted in this
melt-in-your mouth delight.*

Yield: 4 servings

- 4 cups coarsely chopped
  apricots
- 2 tablespoons lemon juice
- 2 cups rolled oats or
  quinoa flakes
- 1/4 cup date sugar
- 1/4 cup sunflower, safflower,
  coconut, or grapeseed oil
- 2 tablespoons water

1. Preheat the oven to 350°F. Lightly oil a 9-inch-square baking dish and set aside.

2. Toss the chopped apricots with the lemon juice and set aside.

3. Combine the rolled oats, date sugar, and oil, and mix well. Remove 1 cup of the mixture and set aside.

4. Add the water to the remaining oat mixture and mix well. Place in the prepared pan and press into an even layer. Cover with the apricots, then top with the reserved oat mixture.

5. Bake for 30 to 35 minutes or until the top is browned and crisp.

6. Serve warm or at room temperature.

CHANGE IT UP . . .

- Instead of apricots, try this recipe with peaches or nectarines.

- For an apricot-blueberry crisp, use 2 cups apricots and 2 cups blueberries.

Perfect Pear Crumble

Both apples and pears work well in this luscious crumble, which can be enjoyed as is or with your favorite sorbet or nondairy ice cream. Try it with a scoop of Acai Sorbet (page 166).

1. Preheat the oven 350°F. Lightly oil a 13-x-9-inch baking dish and set aside.

2. Combine all of the crumble topping ingredients except the oil in a large bowl. Add the oil and stir until evenly mixed. Set aside.

3. Place the pears, raisins, flour, lemon juice, and ginger in a large bowl and mix well. Transfer to the prepared baking dish and spread into an even layer. Sprinkle with the crumble topping.

4. Bake for 45 to 50 minutes or until the pears are tender and the topping is golden brown. Remove from the oven and let sit about 8 minutes before serving.

5. Enjoy warm, at room temperature, or chilled.

Yield: 12 servings

5 cups diced pears, preferably Anjou

$^1/_2$ cup raisins

2 tablespoons oat flour

2 tablespoons lemon juice

1 teaspoon ground ginger

CRUMBLE TOPPING

$1^1/_2$ cups rolled oats or quinoa flakes

$^1/_3$ cup oat flour

$^3/_4$ cup coconut sugar or date sugar

1 tablespoon ground cinnamon

$^1/_2$ cup toasted sunflower seeds (optional)

5 tablespoons safflower, sunflower, grapeseed, or coconut oil

Tropical Cobbler

Pineapples, mangos, and dates create a luscious filling for this yummy cobbler.

Yield: 8 servings

5 cups fresh pineapple cubes

I cup chopped dates

$1/2$ cup diced fresh mango

I tablespoon vanilla

$1/2$ teaspoon ground cinnamon

$1/4$ teaspoon ground nutmeg

$1/4$ teaspoon ground cardamom or allspice

TOPPING

2 cups rolled oats

$1/2$ cup oat flour

$1/2$ cup unsweetened pineapple juice

$1/4$ cup agave nectar or coconut sugar

I teaspoon ground cinnamon

$1/2$ cup safflower oil, sunflower, grapeseed, or coconut oil

1. Preheat the oven to 375°F. Lightly oil an 8-inch square baking dish and set aside.

2. Place the pineapple, dates, mango, vanilla, cinnamon, nutmeg, and cardamom in a medium mixing bowl and stir well.

3. Combine all of the topping ingredients except the oil in another bowl. Add the oil and stir until evenly mixed. Set aside.

4. Transfer the pineapple filling to the prepared baking dish and spread into an even layer. Spread the topping mixture over the filling.

5. Bake for 35 to 40 minutes or until the filling is hot and bubbly and the topping is golden brown.

6. Serve warm, at room temperature, or chilled.

CHANGE IT UP . . .

- For a berry cobbler, substitute blueberries for the pineapple, raspberries for the mango, and unsweetened blueberry juice for the pineapple juice.

- For added texture, include $1/2$ cup toasted sunflower seeds to the topping.

- Substitute the topping mixture with 3 cups Great Gluten-Free Granola (page 165).

Metric Conversion Tables

COMMON LIQUID CONVERSIONS

Measurement	=	Milliliters
1/4 teaspoon	=	1.25 milliliters
1/2 teaspoon	=	2.50 milliliters
3/4 teaspoon	=	3.75 milliliters
1 teaspoon	=	5.00 milliliters
1 1/4 teaspoons	=	6.25 milliliters
1 1/2 teaspoons	=	7.50 milliliters
1 3/4 teaspoons	=	8.75 milliliters
2 teaspoons	=	10.0 milliliters
1 tablespoon	=	15.0 milliliters
2 tablespoons	=	30.0 milliliters

Measurement	=	Liters
1/4 cup	=	0.06 liters
1/2 cup	=	0.12 liters
3/4 cup	=	0.18 liters
1 cup	=	0.24 liters
1 1/4 cups	=	0.30 liters
1 1/2 cups	=	0.36 liters
2 cups	=	0.48 liters
2 1/2 cups	=	0.60 liters
3 cups	=	0.72 liters
3 1/2 cups	=	0.84 liters
4 cups	=	0.96 liters
4 1/2 cups	=	1.08 liters
5 cups	=	1.20 liters
5 1/2 cups	=	1.32 liters

CONVERTING FAHRENHEIT TO CELSIUS

Fahrenheit	=	Celsius
200–205	=	95
220–225	=	105
245–250	=	120
275	=	135
300–305	=	150
325–330	=	165
345–350	=	175
370–375	=	190
400–405	=	205
425–430	=	220
445–450	=	230
470–475	=	245
500	=	260

CONVERSION FORMULAS

LIQUID

When You Know	Multiply By	To Determine
teaspoons	5.0	milliliters
tablespoons	15.0	milliliters
fluid ounces	30.0	milliliters
cups	0.24	liters
pints	0.47	liters
quarts	0.95	liters

WEIGHT

When You Know	Multiply By	To Determine
ounces	28.0	grams
pounds	0.45	kilograms

RESOURCES

For those living with food allergies, the following resources can be invaluable. Along with a list of organizations that offer timely information and support, there are helpful websites, recommended products, and reliable manufacturers that support an allergen-free lifestyle. It is important to note that this list of resources, although extensive, is not complete. Networking and Internet searches will help you discover additional sites, products, and organizations—both established and new.

ORGANIZATIONS

American Academy of Allergy, Asthma & Immunology (AAAAI)
555 East Wells Street, Suite 1100
Milwaukee, WI 53202-3823
414-272-6071
www.aaaai.org
This worldwide nonprofit organization of medical specialists and healthcare professionals is dedicated to "advancement of the knowledge and practice of allergy, asthma, and immunology for optimal patient care." It hosts the largest allergic disease archive in the world.

American Academy of Pediatrics (AAP)
141 Northwest Point Boulevard
Elk Grove Village, IL 60007-1098
847-434-4000
www.aap.org
Dedication to the health and well-being of all infants, children, adolescents, and young adults is the mission of this organization of pediatricians. Contact them for information on all issues relating to children's health. Also provides doctor referrals.

Anaphylaxis Canada
2005 Sheppard Avenue East, Suite 800
Toronto, Ontario M2J 5B4 Canada
416-785-5666
866-785-5660
www.anaphylaxis.org
This non-profit organization was created by and for people with anaphylaxis. Among its many functions, Anaphylaxis Canada provides information and support for people with this hypersensitivity, helping them lead safe, normal lives.

Asthma and Allergy Foundation of America (AAFA)
8201 Corporate Drive, Suite 1000
Landover, MD 20785
800-7-ASTHMA (800-727-8462)
www.aafa.org
Founded in 1953, this not-for-profit organization is dedicated to improving the quality of life for people with asthma and allergic diseases through education, advocacy, and research. It provides practical information, community-based services, and support to patients and families.

Celiac Disease Foundation (CDF)
20350 Ventura Boulevard, Suite 240
Woodland Hills, CA 91364
818-716-1513
www.celiac.org
Since it was founded in 1990, the Celiac Disease
Foundation has championed celiac disease research,
education, awareness, advocacy, and support services.

Food Allergy Research & Education (FARE)
7925 Jones Branch Drive, Suite 1100
McLean, VA 22102
800-929-4040
703-691-3179
www.foodallergy.org
FARE was formed in 2012 as the result of a merger
between the Food Allergy & Anaphylaxis Network
(FAAN) and the Food Allergy Initiative (FAI).
Through world-class research, this organization
is dedicated to "finding a cure for food allergies
and keeping individuals with food allergies safe
and included."

Institute for Responsible Technology (IRT)
PO Box 469
Fairfield, IA 52556
641-209-1765
www.responsibletechnology.org
The IRT is a world leader in educating policy makers
and the public about the health, environmental,
agricultural, and economic risks of genetically
modified (GM) foods and crops.

**National Foundation for Celiac Awareness
(NFCA)**
124 South Maple Street
Ambler, PA 19002
215-325-1306
www.celiaccentral.org
NFCA is a nonprofit organization dedicated to
"increasing diagnoses of celiac disease and other
gluten-related disorders and improving quality
of life for those on a lifelong gluten-free diet."

The University of Chicago Celiac Disease Center
5841 S. Maryland Avenue, Mail Code 4069
Chicago, IL 60637
773-702-7593
www.cureceliacdisease.org
Along with "conducting leading research and providing
education and patient services for celiac disease, The
University of Chicago Celiac Disease Center consists
of a network of doctors who specialize in neurology,
infertility, thyroid disease, dermatology, diabetes,
cancer, and other diseases and disorders that are often
associated with celiac disease. These specialists
collaborate to offer comprehensive diagnosis and
treatment of the disease."

HELPFUL WEBSITES

AllergicChild.com
Created by the parents of a severely food allergic child,
this site offers information, shared experiences, and
practical advice to help keep your food-allergic child
safe and healthy while living a full life. Offers a free
monthly newsletter.

AllergyEats.com
This site provides a user-friendly guide to allergy-
friendly restaurants throughout the United States.
The directory includes over 600,000 restaurants—
large and small—that have been reviewed by people
with food allergies. Also lists allergy-friendly bakeries.

AllergyKids.com
This foundation, whose goal is to protect and restore the
"health of loved ones," offers information on the hidden
dangers in our food supply and the connection to con-
ditions such as allergies, autism, asthma, and ADHD.

AllergyMoms.com
Started by the mother of a child with multiple food
allergies, this website offers coaching sessions for
moms and other caregivers, as well as a free newsletter
with informative articles, allergy-friendly recipes, and
parenting tips.

BabyandKidAllergies.com
This site provides information and links to all things related to allergies, including testing of, recipes for, products for, and much more.

CybelePascal.com
On this site, Cybele Pascal, noted author and mother of a food-allergic family, shares her favorite recipes, as well as tips on new allergen-free products and tidbits from her life with a food allergic family.

Derma.com
This natural skin care line includes products for treating allergic skin reactions.

FoodAllergyKitchen.com
The moderator of this website, which presents extensive allergen-free recipes in all food categories, is the mother of two children with multiple food allergies. The site has been noted as one of the ten best resources for individuals with food allergies.

FoodAllergyTalk.com
In 2003, when she was in the seventh grade, the creator of this site was diagnosed with food allergies. After discovering that information on the subject was relatively scarce at that time, she created FoodAllergyTalk the following year. Geared especially for young people, the site is a means of "sharing information, facts, tips, news, and support to those recently diagnosed with food allergies."

GlutenFree.com
This online resource offers listings of hundreds of brand name gluten-free and wheat-free products, including breads, cakes, prepared meals, and more.

GoDairyFree.org
This informative website offers tips, recipes, and practical advice for those living with milk allergies or lactose intolerance.

HealthyChildren.org
Backed by the American Academy of Pediatrics, this website offers reliable current healthcare information and guidance for parents and caregivers. Includes information on pediatric allergists—their training, the treatment they provide, and how to locate one.

KidsWithFoodAllergies.org
Designed for families raising children with food allergies, this site offers practical information on such topics as reading food labels and making safe food substitutions. It also presents an extensive collection of recipes that are searchable by category and hosts the Parents of Food Allergic Kids (POFAK) Community—the largest online support group for families raising food-allergic children.

LocalHarvest.org
Check this site for a directory of farmers' markets, family farms, and other sources of sustainably grown food in your area.

PeanutAllergy.com
This informative site provides helpful tips, key advice, and links to a host of resources on living with a peanut allergy. Through its forums, you can connect with others to share stories, struggles, and successes. Includes a database of peanut- and nut-free products. Find foods, restaurants, recipes, and much more.

TriumphDining.com
Triumph Dining has "developed the most comprehensive gluten-free restaurant guide in North America, dining cards that help you order gluten free in restaurants where language barriers can make things difficult, and a gluten-free grocery guide to help you find the groceries you need—even if you're traveling and all that's available is a supermarket whose brands you don't know." Offers a free biweekly newsletter with gluten-free recipes, product reviews, and special deals.

waFEAST.org
Washington FEAST (Food Allergy, Eczema, Asthma, and Support Team) is a non-profit advocacy group. Its mission is to educate and support individuals and caregivers who are affected by life-threatening food allergies, and who may also deal with atopic disorders like eczema, and asthma. Provides loads of practical tips and advice.

BRAND NAME PRODUCTS

Amy's
707-568-4500
www.amyskitchen.com
Frozen vegetarian meals; canned beans, soups, chilis. Includes products that cater to those with food allergies or who have other special dietary needs.

Arrowhead Mills
800-434-4246
www.arrowheadmills.com
Extensive selection of organic baking products, including gluten-free flours and baking mixes, grains, seeds, and beans.

Attune Foods
800-641-4508
www.attunefoods.com
Makers of Uncle Sam and Erewhon brand natural, organic, non-GMO cereals and snacks, including many gluten-free varieties. Also producers of Attune brand probiotic chocolate bars.

Authentic Foods
800-806-4737
www.authenticfoods.com
Gluten-free flours and baking mixes for cookies, brownies, breads, pizza and pie crusts, pancakes, and more.

Barbara's Bakery
800-343-0590
www.barbaras.com
Line of gluten-free cereals, cookies, and snacks.

Bob's Red Mill
800-349-2173
www.bobsredmill.com
Full line of gluten-free products, including flours and meals; cereals; mixes for breads, cookies, cakes, pancakes, and pizza dough—all produced in a dedicated facility free from wheat and other gluten-containing grains or derivatives.

Coconut Secret
415-383-9800
888-369-3393
www.coconutsecret.com
Leslie's Organics produces this line of organic, non-GMO coconut products, including coconut sugar, nectar, vinegar, and nondairy desserts, as well as coconut aminos (soy-free soy sauce replacement). Products are gluten-, dairy-, and soy-free.

Daiya
www.daiyafoods.com
Vegan cheese varieties made without soy, dairy, gluten, egg, peanuts, and tree nuts. Extensive line includes mozzarella-, cheddar-, and pepperjack-style shreds; Swiss-, cheddar-, and provolone-style slices; cheddar-, jack-, and havarti-style wedges; and cream cheese-style spreads in a variety of flavors. Ready-made frozen pizzas are also available.

Eden Foods
888-424-3336
www.edenfoods.com
High-quality organic products, including many allergen/gluten-free items, such as oat and rice cereal flakes, rice pasta, soba noodles, freshly ground quinoa flour and brown rice flour, dried fruit, seeds, dried beans, and prepared beans, rice, and chili varieties. All canned products are packaged in BPA-free lined cans.

Ener-G
800-331-5222
www.ener-g.com
Gluten-free, wheat-free, dairy-free, nut-free, and kosher-certified products, including Egg Replacer; cookies, cakes, breads; crackers and snacks; rice pastas.

Enjoy Life Foods
847-260-0300
888-50-ENJOY (888-503-6569)
www.enjoylifefoods.com
*Gluten-free, dairy-free, peanut-free, tree-nut free,
soy-free, egg-free, and casein-free cookies, cereals,
granolas, snack bars, trail mixes, chocolate bars
and chips.*

Follow Your Heart
888-394-3949
www.followyourheart.com
*Soy-, gluten-, and dairy-free varieties of vegan cheese,
salad dressings, and spreads, including Vegenaise—
a mayonnaise alternative.*

Hol-Grain
800-551-3245
www.holgrain.com
*Rice products from America's oldest working rice
mill. Wheat-free/gluten-free rice crackers and baking
mixes; "bread" crumbs made with 100% brown rice.*

Ian's Natural Foods
800-54-FOODS (800-543-6637)
www.iansnaturalfoods.com
*Allergy-friendly meals, snacks, and sides that appeal
to kids—Alphatots (potatoes shaped like letters);
pizza; chicken nuggets, patties, and tenders; mac
and no cheese; French toast sticks; and more.*

Imagine Foods
800-434-4246
www.tastethedream.com
*Rice Dream organic, natural beverages; Rice Dream
frozen desserts.*

Lundberg Family Farms
530-538-3500
www.lundberg.com
*Extensive line of certified organic and eco-farmed
whole grain rice varieties, blends, and products,
including rice cakes, chips, flours, and brown
rice syrup.*

Maple Grove Farms of Vermont
www.maplegrove.com
*Pure maple syrup, maple sugar, and maple sugar
candies; gluten-free pancake and waffle mix.*

NOW foods
888-669-3663
www.nowfoods.com
*Agave nectar, date sugar, organic pure maple syrup
and brown rice syrup.*

Pacific Foods
503-692-9666
www.pacificfoods.com
*Wide variety of allergen- and gluten-free products,
including broths, soups, sauces, rice milk, and
hemp milk.*

Quinoa Corporation
310-217-8125
www.quinoa.net
*Ancient Harvest brand organic, gluten/GMO-free
quinoa grain, flour, flakes, and pastas. Food Merchant
brand ready-made gluten/GMO-free corn polenta.*

So Delicious
866-388-7853
www.sodeliciousdairyfree.com
*Extensive line of coconut milk beverages, frozen
desserts, and "creamers."*

SunGold Foods
800-437-5539
www.sunbutter.com
*SunButter—a peanut butter alternative made from
sunflower seeds.*

Tinkyáda
416-609-0016
888-323-2388
www.tinkyada.com
*Organic rice pasta in a wide variety of shapes
and flavors.*

INDEX

THE ULTIMATE ALLERGY-FREE SNACK COOKBOOK
Over 100 Kid-Friendly Recipes for the Allergic Child
Judi and Shari Zucker

If you have kids, you know how hard it is to find healthy snacks. And if your kids have food allergies, it's even more challenging. Commercially made crackers, chips, and other snack foods tend to be highly processed and loaded with sugar, trans fats, preservatives, and other undesirable ingredients. So what's the solution? How can you provide your child with safe snacks that are not only appealing, but also nutritionally sound?

The Ultimate Allergy-Free Snack Cookbook is designed to help. It provides over 100 vegetarian recipes that are free of eggs, cow's milk, soy, wheat, peanuts, tree nuts, fish, and shellfish. They are also free of gluten and refined white sugar. Best of all, the snacks are wholesome and nutritious—rich in whole grains and fiber, and low in calories. Of course, even the most nutritious foods won't benefit your kids unless they eat them. So the chapters are jam packed with kid-favorite choices—cookies, brownies, chips, pizza, burgers, sorbets, smoothies, and more. But this book is not just about recipes. It also offers helpful tips and support for anyone living with an allergic family. This really is the ultimate snack cookbook!

$15.95 • 144 pages • 7.5 x 9-inch quality paperback • ISBN 978-0-7570-0346-2

THE WHOLE FOODS ALLERGY COOKBOOK
Two Hundred Gourmet & Homestyle Recipes for the Food Allergic Family
SECOND EDITION
Cybele Pascal

The Whole Foods Allergy Cookbook is the first cookbook to eliminate all eight allergens responsible for 90 percent of food allergies. Each and every dish offered is free of dairy, eggs, wheat, soy, peanuts, tree nuts, fish, and shellfish. You'll find tempting recipes for breakfast pancakes, breads, and cereals; lunch soups, salads, spreads, and sandwiches; dinner entrées and side dishes; dessert puddings, cupcakes, cookies, cakes, and pies; and even after-school snacks ranging from trail mix to pizza and pretzels. Included is a resource guide to organizations that can supply information and support, as well as a shopping guide for hard-to-find items.

If you thought that allergies meant missing out on nutrition, variety, and flavor, think again. With *The Whole Foods Allergy Cookbook* you'll have both the wonderful taste you want and the radiant health you deserve.

$18.95 • 240 pages • 8 x 10-inch quality paperback • ISBN 978-1-890612-45-0

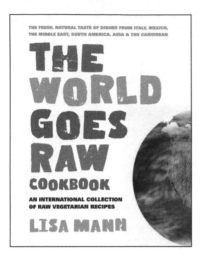

THE WORLD GOES RAW COOKBOOK
An International Collection of Raw Vegetarian Recipes
Lisa Mann

People everywhere know that meals prepared without heat can taste great and improve their overall health. Yet raw cuisine cookbooks have always offered little variety—until now. In *The World Goes Raw Cookbook,* raw food chef Lisa Mann provides a fresh approach to (un)cooking with recipes that have an international twist.

After discussing the healthfulness of a raw food diet, *The World Goes Raw Cookbook* tells you how to stock your kitchen with the tools and ingredients that make it easy to prepare raw meals. What follows are six recipe chapters, each focused on a different ethnic cuisine, including Italian, Mexican, Middle Eastern, Asian, Caribbean, and South American dishes. Whether you are already interested in raw food or are exploring it for the first time, the taste-tempting recipes in *The World Goes Raw Cookbook* can add variety to your life while helping you feel healthier and more energized than ever before.

$16.95 • 176 pages • 7.5 x 9-inch quality paperback • ISBN 978-0-7570-0320-2

EAT SMART, EAT RAW
Creative Vegetarian Recipes for a Healthier Life
Kate Wood

As the popularity of raw vegetarian cuisine continues to soar, so does the evidence that uncooked food is amazingly good for you. From lowering cholesterol to eliminating excess weight, the health benefits of this diet are too important to ignore. Now there is another reason to go raw—taste! In *Eat Smart, Eat Raw,* cook and health writer Kate Wood not only explains how to get started, but also provides kitchen-tested recipes guaranteed to delight even the fussiest of eaters.

Eat Smart, Eat Raw begins by discussing the basics of cooking without heat. This is followed by twelve chapters offering 150 recipes for truly exceptional dishes, including hearty breakfasts, savory soups, satisfying entrées, and luscious desserts. There's even a chapter on the "almost raw." Whether you are an ardent vegetarian or just someone in search of a great meal, *Eat Smart, Eat Raw* may forever change the way you look at an oven.

$15.95 • 184 pages • 7.5 x 9-inch quality paperback • ISBN 978-0-7570-0261-8

For more information about our books,
visit our website at www.squareonepublishers.com